Advance Praise for

Be Your Own Cheerleader

"Neelu Kaur deeply understands the family culture in which Asian and South Asian women are raised and the conflict this poses with the demands of American corporate culture. Her book is an empathetic and realistic guide to navigate this divide so you can have a successful career and a satisfying life. I highly recommend her book!"

—**Shelle Rose Charvet**, Author of the International Bestseller *Words That Change Minds*

"This extraordinary book is a much needed resource for Asian and South Asian women to self-advocate and self-promote not only at work but in all areas of life. I wish I had had this book when I was starting out and I am buying it for every young woman I know."

—**Zarna Garg**, Stand-Up Comedian

"A real-world book of healing and empowerment that addresses both the practical and the spiritual journey of integrating radically different cultures. Neelu Kaur writes from both personal and professional experience, sharing the knowledge and wisdom that is sure to help guide a generation of immigrants."

—**Dr. Marc Halpern**, President of the California College of Ayurveda, Author of *Healing Your Life: Lessons on the Path of Ayurveda*

"*Be Your Own Cheerleader* is much more than a 'how to' for Asian and South Asian women to self-advocate in Corporate America. Ms. Kaur explores the foundational issues that make self-advocacy difficult for women in the workplace—and the special challenges for Asian and South Asian women. She provides her readers with

practical tools and client studies to help explain and explore the means to change the workplace dynamic. It is a thought-provoking, practical, and spiritual journey toward self-realization and self-actualization. A journey every woman in the workplace would do well to experience."
—**Richard J. Haray**, Senior Vice President, The Interpublic Group of Companies

"Neelu Kaur has a deep understanding of working within the corporate environment where cultural influences are perceived as both strengths and weaknesses. With expertise in Organizational Psychology and NeuroLinguistic Programming, she clearly combines information and exercises to help the reader become empowered."
—**Rachel Hott**, PhD, Co-director, The NLP Center of New York

"If you are an Asian or South Asian woman and feel lost in building your career in corporate America, this is an absolute MUST read! Growing up in a family culture of collectivism, Neelu Kaur opens up and speaks with eloquence, candor, and authenticity of encountering her own challenges, heartbreaks, and roadblocks in being her own cheerleader. *Be Your Own Cheerleader* is an invitation for anyone looking for that bridge to succeed in the North American workplace through practical suggestions and advice on self-promotion, advocacy, and thriving!"
—**Bill Hughes**, Partner and Federal Market Leader, CohnReznick, LLP

"A delightful and fascinating guide to becoming your own cheerleader. As someone who coaches people on this very topic, I still learned a lot from Neelu. Get this book—it will change your life!"
—**Noah St. John**, PhD, The Father of AFFORMATIONS® and Founder of SuccessClinic.com

"Neelu's book is a terrific exploration into the cultural, familial, and societal norms that impact the career progression and satisfaction of Asian American women. I was able to relate to so many of the personal stories and situations in the book! Neelu not only provides insight into the behaviors, stereotypes, and misinformation that lead to these scenarios, but shares 'Deliberate Practice' sections to help readers identify and manage these situations in the future. It's a very worthwhile read for any Asian American career woman who wants to understand how to empower herself in the workforce."
—**So Jene Kim**, Partner at Capco

"Neelu has put ancient timeless wisdom into the most practical application of the Self. *Yourself* is a unique expression of cosmic consciousness. Self-knowing is the foundation of life. This book is a practical guide for unfolding our inner awareness in every walk of our life. This book will help every individual to be indivisible, which is an undivided and totally unique expression of awareness."
—**Vasant Lad**, BAM&S, MASc, Founder and Director of The Ayurvedic Institute

"As a South Asian woman, I believe *Be Your Own Cheerleader* is a great resource for Asian and South Asian women to learn the skills for self-promotion and self-advocacy in the workplace. This book can help you regardless of where you are in your career as it's not a skill that comes naturally to us. It's a must read!"
—**Mythili Sankaran**, CEO and Co-founder, Neythri.org

BE YOUR OWN CHEERLEADER

AN ASIAN and SOUTH ASIAN WOMAN'S CULTURAL, PSYCHOLOGICAL, and SPIRITUAL GUIDE to SELF-PROMOTE at WORK

NEELU KAUR

Post Hill
PRESS

A POST HILL PRESS BOOK
ISBN: 978-1-63758-634-1
ISBN (eBook): 978-1-63758-635-8

Be Your Own Cheerleader:
An Asian and South Asian Woman's Cultural, Psychological, and Spiritual
Guide to Self-Promote at Work

Cover design by Conroy Accord

Post Hill Press
New York • Nashville
posthillpress.com

Published in the United States of America
1 2 3 4 5 6 7 8 9 10

To my nani ma (grandmother) Surjit Kaur

TABLE OF CONTENTS

Introduction 11

PART I - KNOW THYSELF

Chapter 1   Raised in the *We*, Thrive in the *I* 17
Chapter 2   Locate Your Motivation 25
Chapter 3   I'm So Proud of You. What?! 32
Chapter 4   Be the Bias Interrupter 39
Chapter 5   What Is Your Interruption Shield? 48
Chapter 6   The Journey from Constraint to Expansion 55

PART II - RETRAIN THE BRAIN

Chapter 7   Change Your Questions and See What Unfolds 63
Chapter 8   Influencing Your Self-Talk 71
Chapter 9   Step into Your Oasis of Inner Resources 82
Chapter 10   Be in Time or Through Time—The
             Choice Is Yours 87
Chapter 11   Who's Really in Charge? 92
Chapter 12   As If... 99
Chapter 13   Flexing the Resilience Muscle 105

PART III - CONNECTING TO YOUR CENTER

Chapter 14   Practicing Inaction 113
Chapter 15   Attachment, Nonattachment, or
             Detachment. How Attached Are You? 119

Chapter 16 Everything Is Operating for You.............................125
Chapter 17 Awareness and Clarity with the Five
            Great Elements...132
Chapter 18 Access Your Powerhouses 144
Chapter 19 The F Word—the Ultimate Cleansing....................152

Closing 161
Letter to the Reader 164
Acknowledgments 168
Appendix 171
    I: Managing Bias and Eight Strategies to Speak Up............173
    II: Global Cross-Country Power Distance Index (PDI)
        Scores 175
    III: Ayurveda...178
About the Author 187

INTRODUCTION

AS AN INDIAN-BORN, AMERICAN-RAISED WOMAN, I was taught to be humble and hardworking, to keep my head down and not draw attention to myself. None of the messaging I received, nor the behavior I observed and modeled for me helped me learn to speak up or get my voice heard. I struggled with self-promotion and advocacy throughout my education and much of my professional career.

Asian and South Asian cultures do not encourage self-promotion. When Asian immigrants or children of Asian immigrants are raised in the United States, they are expected to shed their collective roots and become self-advocates in corporate America. Often, Asian women are overlooked for promotions and do not get credit for their ideas because they are unable to speak up for themselves or their accomplishments. *Be Your Own Cheerleader* helps professional Asian and South Asian women tap into their inner cheerleader and thrive in the North American workplace.

Quiet, submissive, docile, devoted wife, and devoted mother are some (not all) of the stereotypes that Asian and South Asian women fall into. None of these stereotypes support thriving in the individualistic Western workplace. Eastern cultures promote collectivism, where the *We* is cherished and the *I* is nonexistent. Whether you were raised by Asian or South Asian immigrant parents or you migrated to work in the United States from Asian cultures, the expectation is that you know how to speak up for yourself and self-promote at work. This is the first book to help

Asian and South Asian women succeed in the North American workplace. *Be Your Own Cheerleader* is divided into three modules: Cultural, Psychological, and Spiritual. Each module is designed to give Asian and South Asian women different tools in their toolkit to be their own cheerleader at work.

The intention of *Be Your Own Cheerleader* is to help professional Asian and South Asian women, who have toggled between two very different cultures of East and West, thrive in the North American workplace. When you are raised in the collective *We*, it is very difficult to make a name and place for yourself in the individual *I*. Not only are you unskilled in advocating for yourself, but you are also unsure how to be proud of your work or accomplishments.

With the pressures of family perfectionism and shame used as a form of discipline, stress and anxiety are exponentially rising among Asian and South Asian professionals in highly competitive industries across North America. Asian and South Asian women are silent in situations where they need to use a bullhorn because they are unsure and lack the skills to speak up on their own behalf. The scenarios of being overlooked and silenced pile up, causing imposter syndrome and result in a downward spiral of low self-efficacy. It is my mission as an Indian-born, American-raised, South Asian woman to help other women succeed in the Western workplace.

Standing on the shoulders of our Asian and South Asian ancestors, *Be Your Own Cheerleader* is intended to offer a judgment-free perspective on differing components of the East and West. These differences tend to be magnified in the Caucasian-male dominated world of corporate America. Because there are many differing aspects to consider, I focus on the areas that are the most beneficial and salient for Asian and South Asian women, given the information and knowledge I have accumulated in fifteen years of teaching, facilitating, and coaching domestically and internationally in industries ranging from consulting and financial services to technology. I specialize in helping individuals, teams, and organizations be more productive, peaceful, and purposeful at work.

I have a bachelor's degree from New York University's Stern School of Business and a master's degree in social and organizational psychology from Columbia University. I am also a neuro-linguistic programming (NLP) Coach and Master Practitioner. My approach, analysis, and interpretation of various research is at the intersection of leadership and wellness, allowing Asian and South Asian women leaders to be successful in their role while simultaneously addressing mental well-being for themselves and the individuals they manage.

Whether you read this book because you are searching for tools to be your own cheerleader or because you manage, coach, or mentor younger Asian and South Asian women, my wish for you is that you walk away with actionable steps to grab the bullhorn for self-advocacy and self-promotion for yourself and to support those in your spheres of influence.

Part I
Know Thyself

"Knowing yourself is the beginning of all wisdom."

– Aristotle

CHAPTER 1

RAISED IN THE *WE,* THRIVE IN THE *I*

"National Culture cannot be changed, but you should under-stand and respect it."
—Geert Hofstede

IN THE EARLY 2000s, I worked in the consulting industry for one of the top five consulting firms. Typically, consultants worked as a team and traveled together to various companies and client sites. One evening, a senior consultant named Tom asked me to help with research and finalize a presentation that was due the next day. Of course, I had to help and stayed in the office with him until 11:00 p.m. We worked tirelessly to finalize a presentation for a very important meeting the next morning. I felt confident about my contribution and was excited to receive accolades for my work.

I arrived bright and early the next morning, and as I walked into the conference room, the presentation was already underway. *What happened? Did the meeting start early? Did Tom forget to text me and let me know to arrive an hour earlier? Did I oversleep?* My head was spinning with all of the possible scenarios.

Not only did Tom lie about when the meeting started, but he also made no mention of my contribution. He wanted to receive recognition for our collective work without sharing the limelight. We were a team and worked collaboratively, but he decided to take full credit for the work. I didn't know how to speak up and communicate my contribution to the presentation, so I said nothing.

There have been countless times in my life when similar situations have occurred, where I was expected to operate as a *We* and also as an *I*. It's confusing for anyone, but it's even more confusing when you come from a collective culture where the *We* is celebrated and the *I* is shunned.

I first heard about collective and individual cultures in a class in graduate school. Dr. Lee Knefelkamp (lovingly known as Dr. K), was my professor of Intercultural Communications in my master's program at Columbia University. As Dr. K lectured on Hofstede's cultural dimensions, I felt a massive epiphany wash over me. There are a total of six cultural dimensions, but there is one in particular that illuminates a pivotal reason why Asian and South Asian women resist speaking up and self-promoting. We are expected to embrace and reside in the *We* and dim the light on the I. The dimension is referred to as Individualism versus Collectivism.

According to Geert Hofstede, individualism can be defined as a preference for a loosely knit social framework in which individuals are expected to take care of only themselves and their immediate families. Its opposite, collectivism, represents a preference for a tightly knit societal framework in which individuals can expect relatives or members of a particular ingroup to look after them in exchange for unquestioning loyalty.

A society's position on this dimension is reflected in whether people's self-image is defined in terms of the *I* or *We*.[1] The countries that score very high on the individual dimension are the

---

[1]   "National Culture," Hofstede Insights, accessed September 21, 2021, https://www.hofstede-insights.com/models/national-culture/.

United States, Australia, Great Britain, the Netherlands, France, Germany, and other European countries. The countries that score very low on the individual dimension (i.e., considered collective cultures) are India, Japan, Russia, Arab countries, Mexico, and China. Hofstede is by no means implying that everyone in a given society is programmed the same way. There are considerable differences between individuals. However, according to the Intercultural Dimensions, we can still use the research to broadly generalize societal norms of cultures.

How did Individualism versus Collectivism first play out for me? My folks migrated from India to the United States in the late seventies. India is a highly collective society and is based heavily on the *We*, while the United States is a highly individual society and is based heavily on the *I*. My folks wanted to retain the culture of the *We* so much that my brother and I were not allowed to say, "This is my toy." We had to say, "These are our toys." We were taught to share, make decisions as a family unit, and most importantly, worry extensively about what others thought. *What will our relatives say? What will our relatives think about us?*

As I stepped out of the home into other environments (school, my friends' homes, community events, etc.), I consistently danced between the *We* and the *I*. At home, self-identity was not cultivated nor encouraged. The emphasis was on harmony, sharing of resources, and readiness to give up personal interest for the collective interest. Outside the home, the emphasis in school was on self-sufficiency, independence, and placement of self-interest over the collective interest. Confrontation is accepted, whereas in highly collective cultures confrontation is very much avoided.

In elementary and middle school, my teachers would ask, "What do you want to be when you grow up? What do you enjoy doing? What do you love doing?" The questions were interesting to me because they implied I had a choice. My immigrant parents didn't ask these sorts of questions in our home because the assumption was that my brother and I would automatically end up in professions such as engineering, business, or medicine. There wasn't much choice in the matter.

I once wrote an article and it was published in the school newsletter. I was so excited and over the moon to see my name in print that I came running home after school to show the newsletter to my mom. With a look of horror, she exclaimed, "So, you want to be a writer? You are going to write?" Becoming a full-time writer was such a foreign concept that she couldn't wrap her head around choosing a path based on self-fulfillment. Because I didn't know how to advocate for myself, I did not speak up and share my desire to write.

I doubt you will run into many people who truly enjoy or are highly comfortable with confrontation, and I was, in the past, really awful at it, especially in the workplace. I was also ill-equipped to speak up for myself or voice my concerns when I disagreed. There were endless times when my work was overlooked as others on the team took credit for my ideas or deliverables. Remember Tom, the senior team member from the consulting company? The one who not only lied to me about the meeting time but also took credit for my work? I had no idea how to confront him, speak up in front of the client, or advocate for myself.

You might have heard the phrase, "There is no *I* in team." I must say I find it to be completely and utterly untrue. Even among the team at the consulting company, there were folks who were very much comfortable highlighting their inputs and contributions. I'm not here to argue on team versus individual dynamics in corporate America, but what I can absolutely say is that, as a South Asian woman, I needed to learn how to self-promote and be my own cheerleader among the group as I was highly ill-equipped to set myself up for success.

This was the formula for disaster:

Uncomfortable with confrontation + Unable to speak up for myself + Consistently worried about the perception of others = HUGE fail in corporate America

When you come from a *We*-based culture, how do you become comfortable and thrive in an *I* culture? One approach to consider is a concept called *A Part of and Apart From*.

Dancing in and out of the *We* and *I* is no small feat. Looking through the lens of neuro-linguistic programming (NLP), there is a concept of negotiating different *Parts*. Often, there is a need to integrate or negotiate parts of us that are in conflict. When you are raised by parents from a collective culture (e.g., Asia/South Asia) and grow up in an individual culture (e.g., North America), there may be a need to integrate these very different parts. Milton Erickson, founder of Ericksonian hypnosis, used this phrase with his clients: Being a Part of and Apart From. How can you be a part of the group/team and apart from the group/team? In the past, I thought I had to choose one or the other, but after studying Dr. Erickson, I learned that it doesn't have to be either/or; it can be both/and.

An example of Being a Part of and Apart From in a work setting is the ability to collaborate collectively in your team yet own and excel with your individual piece. Taking this one step further, being part of the team and yet apart from the team means not only owning and excelling in your individual piece of the work product, but also communicating your involvement, progress, and attributing credit where credit is due (i.e., credit for YOUR work). Perhaps it's not necessary to communicate your involvement with a bullhorn if that's not your modus operandi, but sometimes, a bullhorn is required to be heard.

In hindsight, I needed to be a part of the collective team effort with Tom but apart from the team, so I should have spoken up in the meeting and shared my contribution. Being a part of the collective team effort meant staying in the office with Tom until 11:00 p.m. and pulling my weight with the research and edits to the presentation. I fell short when being apart from the team. If I could redo that moment when I walked into the presentation, I would have made it clear that the meeting was for a different time on my calendar, and I would have tactfully pointed out my contributions to those in the room. It would have felt uncomfortable to speak up, but it was more detrimental to sit in silence because we teach people how we want to be treated. If I had spoken up in front of Tom, he would have been less likely to repeat the injustice.

It might feel uncomfortable to grab the bullhorn, but the more you do it, the more comfortable it will be to simultaneously be a part of and apart from the team or group.

Deliberate Practice:

Step 1: Sit in a comfortable, cross-legged position on a cushion. If you are sitting in a chair, place your feet on the floor. Spreading out all ten toes, feel your feet firmly grounded.

Keep your spine tall but not rigid. Feel one straight strong line of energy from the crown of your head to your tailbone and from your tailbone to the crown of your head.

Step 2: When you feel ready, gently close your eyes.

Step 3: Relax your jaw and let the tongue rest in the pool of your lower mouth.

Step 4: Bring your attention and focus to your breath. As you inhale, balloon your belly out. As you exhale, bring your belly in toward the spine as if you are giving yourself a hug with the abdomen.

Step 5: Inhale, balloon the belly out. Exhale, belly in toward the spine.

Step 6: Visualize a situation in which you were part of the group and also apart from the group. Was it in a work, family, or social setting? As you focus on the situation, be in the experience and allow yourself to hear what you hear, see what you see, and feel all of the feelings of being a part of a group and yet apart from the group. As you experience the situation, what strategies or tools did you use to be a part of and apart from the group?

Write down any tools, strategies, thoughts, or images you used or had in the experience. Write down anything that comes up for you.

Step 7: Return to the present by breathing deeply into your abdomen (also known as diaphragmatic or belly breathing). Let your jaw relax and tongue rest in the pool of your lower mouth.

Step 8: Imagine a future situation where you will need to be part of and also apart from the group. Take with you anything you gained from the first visualization into this future situation and see how it unfolds.

Step 9: As you begin to open your eyes, know that you are very capable of tapping into this resourceful state of Being a Part of and Apart From whenever you need. You are fully capable because you have done it before. Sometimes we just have to be reminded that we have all of the knowledge and wisdom within us. I invite you to tap into this wisdom and use it in the moments when you need to be a part of a group and apart from the group.

CHAPTER 2

LOCATE
YOUR MOTIVATION

"To know thyself is the beginning of wisdom."

—Socrates

HOW DO YOU KNOW YOU'VE done a good job at a task? Do you have a gut feeling, or do you need someone or something outside of yourself to give validation? Is it a combination? After I facilitate a workshop, I have a feeling or an internal knowing in my body if I performed well; however, I won't fully believe it until I see people smile, hear clapping, or see people rushing toward me to ask questions. During the COVID-19 pandemic, appreciation was available in the chat window for me to reaffirm that I delivered a successful workshop. What does it take for you to know that you've done a good job at a task?

Shelle Rose Charvet is a thought leader in the space of motivation and language patterns. She details five motivation patterns in her book *Words That Change Minds—Mastering the Language of Influence*. There is one in particular that is quite relevant to Asian culture and motivation. It's called the Internal versus External Motivation Pattern.

According to Charvet, "People with an internal pattern provide their own motivation from within themselves. They hold standards somewhere within themselves for the things that are important to them. Their motivation is triggered when they get to gather information from the outside, process it against their own standards, and make judgments about it. Internally motivated people resist when someone tells them what to do or decides for them."[1] The Nike tagline *Just Do It* would not be embraced. They don't want to be told what to do or how to do it because they have a strong sense of what is right and wrong within themselves. I can typically detect when a potential client is internally motivated if they ask specific questions related to their job, role, or organization. I might start the conversation, "Ultimately, you know what's best for your team; my suggestions are xyz." These folks don't want to hear about what I'm working on with my other clients.

Charvet says, "People with an external pattern need other people's opinions, outside direction, and feedback from external sources to stay motivated. They do not hold standards within themselves. They gather them from the outside. Externally motivated people need to compare their work to an external norm or standard, and outside information is taken as a decision."[2] I can typically detect when a potential client is externally motivated if they ask me to share information about other organizations or individuals I coach. One of my clients, Karen, was the head of a compliance division within a large financial services investment bank. She consistently inquired about workshops I facilitated for competitor investment banks. I started conversations with her by saying, "At X and Y companies, I led this workshop, and it was very well-received among the senior managers and directors."

---

1   Shelle Rose Charvet, Words That Change Minds: The 14 Patterns for Mastering the Language of Influence (Institute for Influence, 2019), 49.
2   Charvet, Words That Change Minds, 50.

With any sort of label, we want to rush to judge—is one label better than the other? Is one right or wrong? Absolutely not. According to Charvet, the motivation patterns are differentiators and context-specific. You can be internally motivated with one particular project and externally motivated within your role. You can be externally motivated professionally, and you can be internally motivated in your personal life. The key is to be aware of your pattern to determine if it works for you or if you want to shift based on the context.

In my own experience and when teaching and coaching hundreds of Asian and South Asian women, I noticed that there was an external motivation source pattern with those who were raised by immigrant or first-generation parents from Asia. Because Asian and South Asian cultures are based on group harmony and collective decision-making for the greater good of the group or family unit, there are often many people involved in making a decision. When it comes to academics and career choices, the subtext is that an individual chooses a profession that the family and community accepts. The immigrant mentality is of survival over personal fulfillment.

Raji, a recent graduate from the Massachusetts Institute of Technology (MIT), works for a large tech company. She was born in India and raised in the United States, and she went to an engineering school and became an engineer because her father was an engineer. When I asked her what type of work would be fulfilling, she said she always wanted to be a painter and own her own art gallery. Her choice to go to MIT to become an engineer was based on her father's desire and their community's implicit expectations about acceptable career choices. The opinions of others were the primary motivating factor when making decisions about her life.

Hofstede suggests that collective We-based cultures prefer a tightly knit framework in which individuals can expect their relatives or members of a particular ingroup to look after them in exchange for unquestioning loyalty. Typically, these collective cultures also subscribe to the joint family model where children look after their aging parents. Within Asian culture, there are typically many people residing in the home, and if not, there is still a tight-knit framework and closeness with relatives, which implies many opinions and voices to be heard. When raised in or by parents from a collective culture, there is an external source of validation and motivation embedded in the cultural framework.

Individual cultures promote self-efficiency, where there is a preference for a loosely knit social framework in which individuals are expected to take care of themselves and their immediate families. In individual cultures, tasks come first, and relationships come second. There are fewer cooks in the kitchen, and fewer opinions and voices to be heard. With fewer people providing inputs, individuals are taught at a very young age to rely on themselves and to be self-sufficient. Essentially, they learn to trust themselves and their opinions.

This topic has been a bit controversial as I teach at very large tech companies that are heavily feedback-seeking cultures. They encourage all employees to be in constant feedback-seeking mode for the sake of continuous improvement. I've had people in my class, who had very strong internal motivation sources, say they do not subscribe to feedback-seeking as they have a strong internal compass. Internally motivated people don't like to be told what to do, so if they don't hear anything about their performance, they assume everything is okay. For them, no news is good news, which is why it seems quite unnatural to consistently seek feedback.

There is no right or wrong way to be motivated, and remember that your motivation pattern is context-specific. You can have an internal pattern in one situation and be externally motivated in another scenario. Awareness versus self-critical judgment will allow you to assess where you are on the internal versus external motivation spectrum and decide if you want to choose differently. Personally, I may be at the extreme end of requiring external validation. When I am trying on clothes in a store, I ask a few people for their opinions. In business, I typically operate the same way. Even now, after numerous proposals, I still ask a few trusted advisors for their opinions. After teaching for well over 10,000 hours, I still look forward to the survey results from participants of my workshops and classes to motivate myself. Even if I walked away thinking I taught an amazing class, I won't actually believe it unless I hear clapping or see a slew of positive comments in the chat window of Zoom.

When you come from a collective *We*-based culture where there is an embedded external motivation source, how do you become comfortable and trust your own voice or opinion? Perhaps there are instances where external points of view are required, or there may be instances when you want to trust your own intuition. Identifying where you are and determining if you desire to shift is an empowering way to toggle between the *We* and *I*.

Bora, born and raised in the United States by Korean first-generation immigrant parents, had challenges dancing between the *We* at home and the *I* at work. I explained the difference between the internal and external motivation patterns to her, and she immediately said that at work, she is externally motivated to the point where it is debilitating and prohibits her from meeting deadlines. Digging deeper, we uncovered that in her personal life with her parents, husband, and in-laws, she was also very much externally motivated when it came to making decisions about how to raise her children.

Although her in-laws didn't live in the same home with her, they lived in the same neighborhood to help raise the kids. She consulted her in-laws, parents, siblings, and husband about any decisions relating to her kids. The highly collective, Korean, group consensus culture was bleeding into her individualistic, American-based Wall Street banker job. She found herself constantly seeking validation from colleagues, data, and research, causing her to overanalyze and struggle to complete tasks on time. She wanted to know when she could trust her own judgment and intuition. I coached her to be more reflective and to become aware of her pattern to determine what was most beneficial in a given context. We worked through the practice below on numerous occasions.

Deliberate Practice:

Step 1: Take a moment and reflect. Do you believe you have an internal or external motivation source? If you are unsure of your motivation pattern, answer the following question for yourself:

How do I know that I have a done a good job at XYZ? (Insert specific scenario.)

If you have an internal motivation pattern, the answer will likely be:

> » I decide or know myself.
>
> » I evaluate my own performance based on my own criteria.
>
> » I resist when someone tells me what to do or decides for me.

If you have an external motivation pattern, the answer will likely be:

> » Other people or external sources of information decide or judge for me.
>
> » I need to compare my work to a norm or standard.

Step 2: If you are more internally motivated, ask yourself, "Is that beneficial in the given context?"

If yes, there is nothing to change or do differently.

If you are internally motivated and need to widen your perspective on a deliverable or feedback that you received, consider whose opinion(s) might help you gain new insight. Or perhaps you need to do more research before making a decision. What external sources might you consider?

If you are more externally motivated, ask yourself, "Is that beneficial in the given context?"

If yes, there is nothing to change or do differently.

If you are externally motivated and consistently seek many opinions or rely heavily on external resources, ask yourself, "Do I need multiple opinions or points of reference? How many is enough? Can I trust my own intuition more often?"

Step 3: Wherever you are on the internal versus external motivation spectrum, know that you now have the awareness to identify where you are and the wisdom to behave differently. Your internal compass will guide you to determine if you can rely solely on your intuition or if you need to seek additional external perspectives.

Step 4: Take a moment to pat yourself on the back for learning a new concept that will help you locate your motivation source.

CHAPTER 3

I'M SO PROUD OF YOU. WHAT?!

"We are prepared for insults,
but compliments leave us baffled."
—Mason Cooley

AMERICAN PARENTS ARE PERENNIAL CHEERLEADERS for their children in a way that Asian parents often are not. If you were raised by first-generation Asians or South Asians, you might be able to count on one hand the times you've heard, "I'm so proud of you." In fact, you might have never heard it at all growing up. In Amanda Ripley's book *The Smartest Kids in the World: And How They Got That Way*, she explains that, back in the 1980s and 1990s, American parents and teachers were bombarded with claims that children's self-esteem needed to be protected from competition for them to succeed. The self-esteem movement was quintessentially an American phenomenon. Today, in the United States, the effort and research points to applauding children's efforts rather than their talents.

Typically, in Asian and South Asian cultures, the expectation is to surpassingly exceed every activity you attempt or are interested in. Your folks may have shown in their actions that they were proud of you, just not verbally. Because we didn't hear this often or at all, feeling proud of accomplishments is likely not something you were taught or developed.

I remember when I graduated from Columbia University with my master's in social and organizational psychology in 2009. My family showed their support by being at the graduation ceremony and ultimately helping me pay off the massive education debt I had incurred. On the day of my graduation, my dad said to my mom (roughly translated), "How did she pull this off?"

I interpreted it to mean he was proud of me and didn't know how to communicate it to me directly, but he communicated his pride in actions. My parents never verbalized that they were proud of me because verbal affirmations were a foreign concept and culturally unfamiliar. I couldn't expect them to do something they didn't know how to do, which further perpetuated my inability to be my own advocate and feel proud of my accomplishments. It's difficult to feel proud of yourself when that behavior was not modeled to you as a child.

How do you give yourself a pat on the back when you may not be skilled in doing so?

Practice makes permanent. According to author Tara Lazar, *success* is part of the word *succession*, which means to come after or follow after. We can define success as a succession of small events.[1] Patting yourself on the back, giving yourself credit, and feeling proud of yourself is a muscle, and with our cultural roots, it is not a well-developed one. Celebrating small successes is a great way to

---

[1]   Tara Lazar, Writing for Kids (While Raising Them) (blog), "The Real Meaning of Success," March 29, 2019, https://taralazar.com/2019/05/29/the-real-meaning-of-success/.

build the muscle of self-promotion. Ultimately, once you make this a regular practice, it will be easier to do. Let's start practicing how to acknowledge and celebrate small or large successes and learn to pat yourself on the back.

Deliberate Practice:

Step 1: Reflect on a time when you had a small success. It could be as simple as making it through a difficult day; finishing something on your to-do list that has been lingering for days, weeks, or months; or maybe you hit a minor milestone in a larger project you are working on. Notice one or two, and eventually you will start to notice many small successes throughout your day.

Step 2: Communicate your small wins. If you don't feel comfortable communicating to a friend or coworker, keep a journal of your small wins. It may seem like a silly exercise to write down a small win like completing a difficult day, but eventually you will see pages and pages of small wins.

Step 3: Get excited! Once you are excited, you will begin to establish a practice of noticing and writing down your small wins every day.

Step 4: Acknowledge and reward yourself. Acknowledgment can be as simple as saying it out loud in front of the mirror. "(Insert Your Name), I am so proud of you. Today you did x,y, and z."

A reward could be allowing yourself to take a break after the task is complete or taking a coffee break with a coworker. I will let you get creative with the reward. I trust you know how to reward yourself!

Another aspect of celebrating success is learning how to internalize a compliment. Perhaps you experience a sense of discomfort with verbal affirmations or receiving compliments from others. I've seen and experienced this with many of the Asian and South Asian women I coach and teach. It's actually something that is still challenging for me, but I am fortunate to be able to practice frequently.

When I receive compliments on the way I deliver a class or with coaching clients, there is an initial sense of uneasiness. The good news—or actually the great news—is that, with awareness, you can coach yourself to internalize the compliment. Internalizing a compliment is the ability to take a compliment to heart and let it nourish and provide feelings of positivity toward yourself. There may be an initial sense of discomfort, but if you take a moment to identify the emotion or sensation you are experiencing, you will decrease the magnitude of the uneasiness.

"Name it to tame it" is a phrase coined by Dr. Daniel Siegel. Essentially, by naming the emotion you are experiencing, you can tame the magnitude of the feeling. For example, I might internally say, "I am experiencing uneasiness receiving this compliment" or "I feel a tight ball of nerves in my stomach." According to Dr. Siegel, choosing words to describe subtle emotions jumpstarts your executive brain and calms down the emotional limbic brain. Naming the emotion gives your brain time to filter and organize your reaction.

Now, it's time to internalize the compliment. How do you allow yourself to be receptive to receiving a compliment when you are not accustomed to do so? In psychotherapy, it's referred to as the inability to accept positive affect. The issue for many of us is related to feeling somewhere deep inside that we don't deserve the praise. We might believe we are not worthy to take in the experience of feeling good about ourselves, or we struggle to believe someone else feels good about us. We all have an inner critic and the beautiful thing about this inner critic is that it is there to help us in some way.

In the field of Neurolinguistic Programming (NLP) there is a basic premise that every behavior has a positive intention. Even a behavior that has negative consequences (feeling bad or uneasy) has a positive intention. For example, if you have an inner critical voice about being an imposter in your job, the positive intention could be a desire to keep striving for excellence or to provide motivation to continue working at proving your value in the organization. In the past, when I first started my own business and I had a potential client that fell through, my inner critic sent me in a downward spiral, providing images of losing my apartment and a voice saying, "You are all alone...how will you survive?"

I used to get upset with myself for having those thoughts. Slowly, over time, I learned to thank this scared inner critic for her concern about keeping me safe, fed, and sheltered. Now I say, "Thank you for sharing, but I will be okay." The journey to becoming your own cheerleader requires internalizing a compliment and befriending your inner critic.

Deliberate Practice:
Acknowledging and Befriending your Inner Critic:

Step 1: Reflect on a time when you received a compliment, but you were not able to take it in. You might have responded to the person who gave you the compliment with a return compliment, or you might have simply brushed it off. Whatever your response was, take a moment and reflect on it. Who was it from? What did they say to you?

Step 2: If there was an inner critic present or if an internal negative dialogue came up, what was the message? What did your inner critic say to you? Write down your answer if you are more visual, or say it out loud if you are more auditory.

Step 3: Take a moment and, with genuine curiosity, think about the positive intention of your inner critic. Was it to protect you or to keep you safe? Whatever the reason, take a moment and identify your inner critic's positive intention. Write down your answer if you are more visual, or say it out loud if you are more auditory.

Step 4: Show compassion to your inner critic. Actually, thank your inner critic by identifying the positive intention. The healing process happens simply by showing compassion to your inner critic with a desire to understand the positive intention.

Now, let's actually allow ourselves to feel good. Take it all in!

Internalizing a Compliment:

Step 1: Reflect on a time you received a compliment that was meaningful to you. If you are having a hard time remembering a compliment you received, think of conversations where you might have glossed over the compliment. If you are still having trouble thinking of a time, perhaps look through your text messages or on your social media page(s) or timeline. I'm positive someone has complimented you!

Step 2: Close your eyes and imagine hearing the compliment from the person. Allow yourself to step into the moment you received the compliment. Hear what you hear, see what you see, and feel everything you feel as you allow yourself to take in the compliment.

Step 3: Allow yourself to bask in the compliment. Really allow yourself to sit with the compliment even if it may feel uncomfortable in the beginning. Take in the compliment and be in the experience fully.

Step 4: Open your eyes and give yourself a pat on the back for receiving the compliment fully! Practice this as much as you can because practice makes permanent. Remember: If someone gives you a compliment, resist the urge to turn around and give back a compliment. Don't hand it right back to them.

CHAPTER 4

BE THE
BIAS INTERRUPTER

*"When dealing with critics always remember
this: Critics judge things based on what is outside of their content of understanding."*
—Shannon L. Alder

I WAS BORN AND RAISED as a Sikh. I studied Hinduism thoroughly through my education in yoga and Ayurveda, and my curious nature led me to an extensive study of Buddhism and Kabbalah. All of these religions/philosophies say we were born into this body and era for a reason. The reason could be to deal with past life karma or to learn and make corrections in this life to set us up for the next life. Whatever your spiritual beliefs are, I'm sure there are times when you may wonder why you arrived in this lifetime as an Asian or South Asian being raised a collective culture like the United States/North America. I don't know the answer for you, but I do know that there is a reason you are here in this body with this hair color and this skin color.

With this body, hair, and skin color comes generalizations, stereotypes, and, often in the workplace, many other biases we must face. A stereotype is defined as a fixed or overgeneralized belief about a particular group of people. One advantage of a stereotype is that it enables us to respond quickly to situations because we have had similar experiences in our past. One disadvantage is that it makes us ignore differences between individuals, leading us to make broad generalizations about groups of people.

An example of how I experienced this in my own life was when I worked closely with a financial consulting company based on Wall Street. They hired me to assist with curriculum design and deliver trainings across all of their offices in North America. I was rated one of their top facilitators. In fact, my ratings surpassed Sarah, an internal learning and development manager.

Sarah became very uncomfortable and intimidated when I received accolades for my classes. We were meeting with a senior partner, and she said, "It must be nice to come from a wealthy, educated family and go to an Ivy League school." Yes, there are absolutely Indians that come from wealthy, educated families. I do not happen to be one of those Indians. My parents are immigrants who arrived in the United States with an eight-year-old and a two-year-old (me) in tow. They had no formal education and arrived with a whopping seventy-five dollars.

When she made this statement, I took a couple of deep breaths, gathered myself, and responded by debunking the stereotype that not all Indians come from wealthy, educated families. I explained my background and how I had to work very hard for my Ivy League education. Sarah then opened up about her family's humble, Italian-immigrant, blue-collar roots from Yonkers, New York. By overtly surfacing the unconscious bias, we were able to find a common denominator in our immigrant backgrounds.

I'm sure you are well aware of some of the typical Asian or South Asian stereotypes like our homes smelling of curry or other Asian aromas, being excellent in math and science, or being the model minority. There are so many out there that there is no need for me to elaborate further as I'm sure you are well acquainted with many more. By the way, I am definitely not good with mathematics. I use my phone to calculate the simplest arithmetic, but there are a whole host of other things that I do extraordinarily well. You may fall into one or many of the stereotypes, or you may not. If you don't fall into a particular stereotype, it is absolutely okay. You are an individual with an individual story. If you do fall into a stereotype, it might just allow you to have a good laugh.

As a non-Black woman of color, I have experienced both overt and covert racism in the workplace. If left unexamined or unaddressed, the scenarios pile up, potentially causing imposter syndrome that results in a downward spiral of low self-efficacy. With low self-efficacy and a sense of exclusion and non-belonging in an organization or team, you are less likely to use a bullhorn to advocate for yourself.

Because we are women, our work will often be unseen or someone else will attempt to take credit for our genius. Being Asian or South Asian women, we may need to add a microphone to the bullhorn because we are an underrepresented population in corporate America. In an effort to add a microphone to your bullhorn, I will focus on a simple strategy to address implicit bias against Asians and South Asians in the workplace. But first, we need to understand implicit bias. Once addressed, it's much easier to self-advocate.

The difference between stereotypes and implicit bias is that implicit or unconscious biases are outside of conscious awareness. Biases are implicit drivers that influence how we experience the world. They are adaptive mechanisms that enable quick decisions with minimal cognitive effort. There are benefits and downfalls of implicit biases. Because our brains are very complex and processing so much information constantly, implicit or unconscious biases allow for mental shortcuts, which can be efficient. Unfortunately, efficiency does not mean accuracy!

The brain learns from past experiences and information we have gathered from others, and it uses this previously collected data in new contexts. By virtue of having a brain, we are biased because we are hardwired for automatic processing. Unfortunately, what may occur is that we use biases as mental shortcuts to make decisions about individuals based on past data. My work with Sal showed how these mental shortcuts can be problematic.

Sal, a United States–born Italian-American, managed a team of engineers and product managers at a large tech company. In a previous role at a different organization, he had managed a similar type of team where he had a negative experience with one of his senior engineers, who was a Chinese woman. Because of this challenging relationship, he used past data to make hiring decisions for his current team and avoided hiring Chinese women. We can't fault Sal for carrying forward memories of a negative experience; however, using past data about an individual in a current situation is a disservice to team diversity and inclusion. Our coaching sessions focused on Sal learning strategies to surface and counteract his implicit biases.

For a number of years, I taught a class called Managing Unconscious Bias in large tech and financial services organizations. A question I was frequently asked was, "What do I do when a bias is used against me?" Let me first remind you of the airplane oxygen mask analogy for self-care: Put the oxygen mask on yourself first before taking care of anyone else. It can be an alienating and triggering experience to be on the receiving end of an Asian or South Asian bias. When we are the target of the bias, we must put the oxygen mask on ourselves first, so we can respond resourcefully.

Dr. Lisa Feldman Barrett, a neuroscientist and author of *How Emotions Are Made,* has an empowering approach about the concept of our brain being triggered or our amygdala being hijacked. Barrett suggests that our emotions are based on a body budget. This body budget is composed of water, salt, glucose, and other resources that keep a person alive and well. She suggests that, in moments when we are triggered, we need to check in and see if our body budget is at a deficit. Do we need to hydrate, eat, take a nap, jog around the block, call a friend, or simply take a deep breath? When our body is running a deficit of the resources it requires for optimum functioning, we will likely respond in a manner we might regret later.

I've spent a lot of time pondering how to use this body budget approach in the moment when I'm triggered, outraged, or angry because someone has made a derogatory comment about immigrants. As it relates to implicit or unconscious bias, when we are the target, we definitely don't want to respond while in a body budget deficit.

If you are the target of implicit or unconscious bias in written communication, you might notice you are frantically typing your response and tempted to hit send immediately. If you are communicating face-to-face or via video conference, you might not be able to think rationally because you are so upset. When in this emotionally triggered state, you may respond defensively, shut down, or even worse, say something you will regret later.

What can you do? Dr. Barrett suggests checking in with yourself and asking, "What do I need in this moment?" You may need to step away, take a few deep breaths, eat, hydrate, or do something else. In instances where you cannot walk away or reschedule, the easiest way to reset is through slowing down the breath. Taking a few deep long breaths buys you time, gets the blood flowing to the brain, and allows you to respond rationally.

Because breathing is an autonomous process, many people don't think about it (unless of course you are a yogi). The breath initiates an immediate return to the present moment. There are a whole host of other strategies to become resourceful in the moment, but I believe a pause and a deep breath is the easiest anchor to access in an emotionally-triggered moment. Breath control is also known as pranayama. *Light on Pranayama* by B.K.S. Iyengar provides various types of pranayama. To keep it simple, I am going to guide you through the most basic: Deep Abdominal Breathing (also known as Belly Breath).

Deliberate Practice:

Step 1: As you inhale, balloon the belly out. Fill up the lungs with air, and breathe into your abdomen, diaphragm, and chest. If that is too much to remember, just take a deep breath in while you balloon the belly out.

Step 2: As you exhale, bring the belly in toward the spine. It's almost as if you are giving yourself a hug with your abdomen.

That's it! It's that simple. Take some deep breaths with the belly, and let at least six seconds pass with no reaction.

Now that the six seconds have passed, there are three aspects to consider: Self-care, Depersonalization, and Confrontation.

Self-care: Stopping the negative impact of the unconscious bias on your self-esteem

When you find yourself in a situation where you are on the receiving end of an implicit or unconscious bias, chances are the other person is not aware they have offended you or have said something that is biased. Remember that these implicit biases are operating unconsciously, so it's nothing against you personally. Before you bring it to their attention, you might want to manage your own psychological and emotional state first. Remind yourself that it has absolutely nothing to do with you. This person is using past history with other Asians or South Asians to make a decision about you. It has nothing to do with you or your performance. You may feel off-center or off-balance; to arrive at a more centered and grounded state, simply ground your feet into the earth. Then choose a mantra to repeatedly say to yourself like, "This has nothing to do with me."

Depersonalization: Be the bias interrupter

In Buddhism, there is a famous quote: "Holding on to anger is like grasping a hot coal with the intent of throwing it at someone else; you are the one who gets burned." Being angry at the other person is not going to help the situation. In fact, it can damage the relationship, and you don't want to damage the relationship with a manager or co-worker when you have to interact with them every day. It may be really difficult to do it in the moment, but try to remind yourself that this person is unaware of the bias, so assume positive intent.

You want the other person to be aware of the bias so it doesn't impact any decisions about you or your work. You also want to pave the way for all other Asians and South Asians, so it's crucial that you speak up and be a bias interrupter. However, the way you interrupt is of paramount importance. A bias interrupter is someone who brings to surface the implicit bias without attempting to eliminate the bias, but to simply raise conscious awareness that the bias exists. Interrupting a bias is most successfully done after a few deep breaths when you are not triggered or activated and can think rationally and respond resourcefully. In the diversity, equity, and inclusion space, there are various strategies suggested on ways and language to use to interrupt biases. I've included one simple strategy here. There are additional strategies in the Appendix.

Confrontation: Paraphrase or repeat back what they said

When restating the bias, it allows the other person to reflect and hear out loud what they said. Your tone of voice is important as you are not trying to ridicule. Your intent is to understand and clarify.

It may be something like this: "So are you saying all Asians are good in math and science and should become engineers?"

By virtue of saying it out loud, the other person might realize that what they said is a broad generalization and not true for every individual. If it's still not registering, you may need to go a step further and explain why the broad generalization is not applicable to you and many other Asians and South Asians. Remember to assume positive intent and that the other person truly does not know they said something that is untrue or, worst case, offensive.

I am oversimplifying because managing Asian and South Asian bias in the workplace could be an entire book. The key takeaway is that, when interrupting a bias, the goal is not to eliminate the bias, but to bring it to surface, so the other person is consciously aware of it. This will provide an opportunity to speak up for yourself and pave the way for other Asians and South Asians who may journey down the same path in the future.

CHAPTER 5

WHAT IS YOUR INTERRUPTION SHIELD?

"Your silence will not protect you."
—Audre Lorde

MY JAW TIGHTENED, MY SHOULDERS slumped, and I felt an intense fluttering sensation in the pit of my stomach. My inner voice questioned on repeat, "Why is this happening?!" I was in a meeting early in my career where I was presenting key findings to a senior management team, and the loudest voice in the room kept interrupting me. He was questioning my suggestions in an abrasive manner without waiting for his turn to speak. At that time, I felt hopeless and a sense of despair whenever someone interrupted me. I would beat myself up and wonder why I was continuously interrupted mid-sentence. The frequency of these abrasive cut-offs has decreased substantially, but it still happens. Even now, with all of my credentials, experiences, and tenure in corporate America, I still get interrupted, but my inner questioning has shifted to, "What can I do in this moment?"

A study from George Washington University found that men interrupted women 33 percent more often than they interrupted other men. Over the course of a three-minute conversation, men interrupted women 2.1 times. In contrast, during conversations of the same duration, men interrupted other men only 1.8 times. Women on average interrupted men only once.[1] Based on my own experiences and those of women I have coached, Asian and South Asian women experience these disruptive interjections more frequently than other women of color. I can't find statistics to back up this hypothesis; however, I have more than two decades of experience working in corporate America and over fourteen years of experience coaching Asian and South Asian women, and I've seen this happen a lot. Yan is one of my clients who struggled with consistent interruptions when speaking at work.

An independent consultant with over twenty years of experience in the tech industry, Yan was born and raised in San Francisco. Her parents are immigrants from China, and she is the first in her family to graduate from college and graduate school. Yan started her career as a junior project manager in San Francisco at one of the largest tech companies. In this role, she worked with male engineers who often cut her off when she was speaking. They discounted her opinions and constantly interrupted her mid-sentence. She struggled to get a word in and felt drained by the amount of effort it took to be heard, so eventually, she accepted that she was going to have to get used to frequent interruptions. Yan struggled to find her voice.

Why might Asian and South Asian women like Yan have a hard time jumping into the conversation and speaking up? I attribute one of the reasons to the Power Distance Index (PDI) from Hofstede's cultural dimensions. According to Hofstede, "PDI is defined as the dimension that expresses the degree to which less powerful members of society accept and expect that power is dis-

---

1   "How often are women interrupted by men? Here's what the research says," Advisory Board, July 7, 2017, https://www.advisory.com/daily-briefing/2017/07/07/men-interrupting-women.

tributed unequally. People in societies exhibiting a large degree of Power Distance accept the hierarchical order in which everybody has a place and which needs no further justification. In societies with low Power Distance, people strive to equalize the distribution of power and demand justification for inequities of power."[2] In other words, if you come from or grew up in a culture with a large degree of Power Difference, you are more likely to accept and not question a hierarchical order of power.

Asian and South Asian countries score high on the PDI. In fact, all score above 50.[3] (See the Appendix for a cross-country comparison between the United States and Asian countries.) What does the PDI score mean? A culture that gives great deference to persons of authority has a high PDI score, and a culture that values the equal treatment of everyone has a lower PDI score. For example, the United States has a PDI score of 40, whereas China scores 80. This means that, in the United States, there is less of a hierarchical order of authority than in China. In China, hierarchy and power structures are accepted, but in the United States, they are very much challenged.

In Asian and South Asian cultures, there is reverence for the elderly. There is embedded respect in our cultures for those who have more life experience and wisdom. When I was growing up, for example, it was unacceptable to question or talk back to my folks or other older family members. If I ever did, there would be turmoil in the home. There was a hierarchical order in my family, and I just had to accept that. Questioning it would only disrupt group harmony. With this Power Distance in the backdrop of my subconscious, I entered into the workplace assuming everyone knew more

---

2   "National Culture," Hofstede Insights, accessed September 21, 2021, https://www.hofstede-insights.com/models/national-culture/.

3   "National Culture," Hofstede Insights, accessed April 10, 2022, https://www.hofstede-insights.com/country-comparison/.

than I did and was more senior, so I wasn't well-versed in speaking up when interrupted. Because I was so unskilled in speaking up, when I did muster up enough courage to jump into a conversation, I often appeared defensive or had an angry tone of voice. At that time, I didn't know how to gracefully and tactfully thread myself back into a conversation.

Imagine sitting across from your manager during a performance review and not being able to represent yourself appropriately because you keep getting cut off. Or you are in a high-stakes presentation with key colleagues, it's a defining moment in your career, and the loudest voice in the room constantly interrupts you. Or at a client meeting, you are asked to introduce yourself to a new team you will be working with, and the internal partner continuously chimes in, pushing his own agenda. These are all situations where grabbing the bullhorn is necessary because your personal brand is at stake. If you are silenced too often, no one will hear what you have to say, and that could be interpreted as lack of competence or indifference. Neither interpretation will lead you to your next promotion or career advancement.

Through my own experiences and coaching Asian and South Asian women, I've noticed two types of interruption scenarios that frequently occur:

1. Someone interrupts you as you are speaking, and you struggle to jump back in the conversation.

2. You need to interrupt someone or a group discussion to get your point across.

In both of these scenarios, there are phrases that might make interjecting a bit smoother. These Interruption Shields are phrases you can etch in your memory. You can use them over and over again to avoid getting triggered if you are being interrupted or can't get a word in. When using any of these Interruption Shield phrases, be mindful of your tone so you don't come across as defensive or angry.

In the first scenario, when someone interrupts you and you want to jump back into the conversation with ease, some Interruption Shield phrases could be:

"I'd like to circle back..."

"If I may just complete that thought..."

"I'd love to finish my thought before we move on..."

"Oh, really quick, I would like to finish my thought here..."

"Hold on one sec, I want to finish my thought..."

"Just a sec, I'd like to finish my thought..."

"I'm excited to hear the next item, but I'd love to finish my thought here..."

"Hold on. Let me wrap this thought..."

"I'm not finished; may I continue..."

"One more thing..."

"Please allow me to finish..."

"If you don't mind letting me finish, I'd love to hear what you have to say..."

In the second scenario, when you need to interrupt to get your point across, some Interruption Shield phrases could be:

"May I..."

"May I interject here..."

"If I may comment here..."

"Can we hit pause; I have a thought..."

"Hold on, I need to jump in here..."

"Excuse me, I have a point to add..."

"I must interject here..."

"One sec, I need to add something..."

"I need to make a point here..."

"One thing we are missing is..."

"Something else to consider..."

"Did we also consider..."

Some of the Interruption Shield phrases may sound too formal or informal given your environment. Choose the phrases that work for you and your context. Always know your audience and find the phrase(s) that resonate with you. This approach helped Yan find her voice.

Yan and I reconnected after she left the project management job where she first struggled with speaking up. She worked in a few other organizations before realizing she wanted to start her own consulting company. If she was going to be out on her own, she knew she needed to stand her ground in sales conversations. Yan created an incredible website and had all of her ducks in a row to pitch her services. However, it was still challenging for her to get back in a conversation when a potential client interrupted her to ask questions, share their opinion, or disagree with her approach. We worked together on developing Interruption Shield phrases based on the scenarios above. She has been practicing her Shield phrases for years and now feels much more confident, so she can stay present and unrattled when interrupted.

Deliberate Practice: (journal practice)

Step 1: Sit in a comfortable position and take a few deep breaths. Allow yourself to settle in with your breath.

Step 2: Think about a time in the past when you were interrupted. How did you feel? What sensations did you experience in your body? Locate where you felt that sensation. Write down anything that is coming up for you.

Step 3: As you reflect on this moment when you were unheard and cut off, write down any Interruption Shield phrases that resonate with you.

Step 4: Practice saying the phrase(s) out loud.

Step 5: Shake it out.

Step 6: Take a moment to take a few deep breaths and settle back in with your breath.

Step 7: Think about a time in the past where you needed to interject but you didn't know how or what to say.

Step 8: As you reflect on this moment when you stayed silent, write down any Interruption Shield phrases that resonate with you.

Step 9: Practice saying the phrase(s) out loud.

Step 10: Shake it out.

Remember this is something that must be practiced over and over again for you to find your voice. Now that you've identified the Interruption Shield phrases that resonate with you, begin practicing in every opportunity you are given.

CHAPTER 6

THE JOURNEY FROM CONSTRAINT TO EXPANSION

"Take up space. Do not minimize your-self for the convenience of others."

—Tonya Ingram

ALTHOUGH AMERICAN WOMEN HOLD 52 percent of all management and professional jobs, they lag substantially behind men in terms of representation in leadership positions.[1] The sad truth is that this is the case across many industries, including the law, medicine, academia, and financial services. In financial services, only 12.5 percent of women are Chief Financial Officers (CFOs) in Fortune 500 companies.[2] At the intersection of gender and race, Asian and South Asian women struggle even further with representation in leadership roles. In the tech industry, only 1

---

1   "Labor Force Statistics from the Current Population Survey: Employed persons by detailed occupation, sex, race, and Hispanic or Latino ethnicity," U.S. Bureau of Labor Statistics, accessed November 2018, http://www.bls.gov/cps/cpsaat11.htm.
2   Claire Zillman, "With First Woman CFO Dhivya Suryadevara, GM Enters Rare Fortune 500 Territory," Fortune, June 14, 2018, http://fortune.com/2018/06/14/dhivya-suryadevara-gm-cfo/.

in 285 women is an executive.[3] Asians and South Asians experience career setbacks because of lack of role models and expectations of timidity.

Being timid and not having the skillset to speak up has held back Asian and South Asian women in the workplace. In order to be the role models for future generations, it starts with self-analysis and exploration. As children, we unconsciously modeled behaviors of those around us. Did the women in your life speak up for themselves? Were they fearful to say or do something that would negatively affect the family dynamics? Were your parent(s) so concerned with what others in the community thought that the goal was to present the family in the most positive light without drawing attention to any one particular member? If the answer to any or all of these questions is a resounding *Yes!*, then you likely have memories of being told to follow cultural norms, and you may have observed the women in your life taking up as little space as possible.

As we learn to take up space, speak up, and advocate for ourselves, we will be better equipped to not only be our own cheerleaders in professional and personal settings, but also assist future generations to add a microphone to their bullhorn for self-promotion. We are paving the way for all of the Asian and South Asian women who may be on the trail directly behind us. They are observing our behaviors and searching for role models and mentors.

Because it's quicker to change the mind with the body than it is with the mind, let's examine how to change our physiology to inhabit more space. Amy Cuddy, the bestselling author of *Presence*, discusses the impact of body language on emotional states.[4] Her

---

3   "Often Employees, Rarely CEOs: Challenges Asian-Americans Face in Tech," NPR, May 17, 2015, https://www.npr.org/2015/05/17/407478606/often-employees-rarely-ceos-challenges-asian-americans-face-in-tech.

4   "Does Body Language Shape Who You Are?," NPR, December 13, 2013, https://www.npr.org/transcripts/248198314.

research of power poses arose from her analysis of animals. Power poses are postures that are open, expansive, and occupy physical space.

Physiologically, when we take a wide stance—chest out, hands on hips, leaning back, or putting hands behind your head with elbows out—there is a hormonal change in the body. Just like animals, when human beings take these powerful expansive poses, testosterone levels increase and cortisol levels decrease. Because we can change our minds faster with our bodies than with the mind, you can alter the physiological makeup in the body by taking a power pose. You gain confidence with the increased testosterone and decrease stress levels with the lowered cortisol level in the body.

Power poses are helpful when you anticipate a potential stress-inducing situation. You can change your emotional state by becoming more expansive with the body. Prior to facilitating any in-person workshops or entering the stage for speaking engagements, I would find a bathroom stall and become big and expansive with my body. At a staggering 5'4", I don't need a large space to expand! By virtue of becoming more open and expansive with my body, I became more confident. During the COVID-19 pandemic, I created a similar ritual before I turned the camera on for a video call. It's really that simple. You can gain confidence and decrease stress levels in the body with power poses. Let's practice.

Deliberate Practice:
Feel Power in the Body with a Power Pose

Step 1: Take a moment to contract your body. Get small, hunch down, round the back, and become constrained in your body. Notice how you feel in your body and emotionally.

Step 2: Shake it out!

Step 3: Now, get as big and expansive as you possibly can with your body. If you are sitting in a chair, lean back and open out your arms with your elbows wide. If you are standing, elongate your spine, widen your stance, and take a deep long breath. Take a moment and notice how you feel in your body and emotionally.

Step 4: Shake it out!

Step 5: Next time you are presenting, speaking in a large group, or facilitating a meeting, take a moment or two prior to the event to make a big expansive posture with your body.

When you have time to prepare or if you are anticipating that you will need a boost of confidence, making a power pose can be a way to change your physiological state. What happens if you find yourself in a situation where you can't make a power pose? Maybe you are in a meeting and something has upset you. Perhaps someone is speaking over you or you are having a hard time finding your voice. What if you need to tap into that wellspring of calm and confidence simultaneously?

Riddhi, an Indian-born, American-raised, mid-level executive in the telecom industry, experienced years of being spoken over in meetings. She wanted to be polite and respectful and not cut anyone off from speaking. With the most noble intention of allowing her colleagues the space and room to share their opinions, she felt she was creating the opposite experience for herself. Riddhi felt like her voice was not heard. She felt like her opinions were inconsequential, and she felt silenced in meetings where her input was crucial. I worked with Riddhi on a two-part process of centering within herself and expanding her energy and presence, so she could practice in the moment.

This centering exercise is from Wendy Palmer and Janet Crawford's work in *Leadership Embodiment* where she combines Aikido and mindfulness. (Wendy Palmer has approved the inclusion of this exercise.)

Deliberate Practice: Centering and Grounding in the Moment 20-Second Centering from Wendy Palmer and Janet Crawford's *Leadership Embodiment*

Step 1: Focus on Breath—As you inhale, uplift your posture and lengthen your spine. Slowly exhale downward toward the earth (take twice as long as your inhale), softening your jaw and shoulders as you go down.

Step 2: Relate to Gravity—Gravity is your natural way to relax. Feel the weight of your body in your arms pulling your shoulders away from your ears and relaxing the tension in your jaw. Allow gravity to settle you into your personal space and onto the earth.

Step 3: Balance Personal Space—Ask yourself, "Is the back of my personal space balanced and even with the front of my personal space? Is the left equal to the right? And is above equal to below?" Expand your personal space to fill the room.

Step 4: Evoke a Quality—Your quality represents something you want to cultivate in yourself. Working with a quality is a practice of inquiry. "If there was a little more _____ (confidence, expansion, ease, etc.) in my body, what would that be like?" If there was 5 percent more of that quality, what would that feel like? Where would I notice the quality in my body?

Part II
Retrain the Brain

"There is no such thing as failure, only feedback."

– NLP Presupposition

CHAPTER 7

CHANGE YOUR QUESTIONS AND SEE WHAT UNFOLDS

"It is not the answer that enlightens,
but the question."

—Eugène Ionesco

MIKA, A JAPANESE-BORN AND AMERICAN-RAISED senior sales specialist, worked for a large tech company based in Chicago. She spent twelve years in the financial services industry and decided to transition to tech because she wanted a more challenging environment. Mika was the only Asian American on the sales team and also felt she had a huge learning curve as it related to understanding the nuances of the tech industry. She was experiencing debilitating imposter syndrome to the point where she was questioning her choice to leave financial services. Unsure of her skills and feeling isolated as the only Asian on the team, she began to fall prey to her destructive, negative, inner dialogue. Many of us know how hard it can be to struggle with an inner critic.

Alongside being a super rock star in your role at work, your other job—and actually the most important job you will ever have—is to manage your mental health. This is no easy task and takes constant vigilance of what you allow in and out of your precious mind. The other piece of mental health management that is quite challenging to control is the internal dialogue you have with yourself. The inner critic can run the show and your job is to make sure you keep it in check. The inner critic doesn't rule the show; you do. You ultimately have a choice: Are you going to work for your inner critic or are you going to manage and lead your inner critic? Empowerment comes from a place of managing the negative inner dialogue.

The best place to start is with the questions you ask yourself. In *Change your Questions, Change Your Life*, Dr. Marilee Adams talks about the Judger and the Learner mindset. She states that we have both mindsets, but we have the power to choose where we will operate from in any moment. The Judger mindset is judging self and others, whereas the Learner mindset is accepting self and others. The Judger is in the either/or thinking, whereas the Learner is in the both/and thinking. The types of questions you ask yourself will allow you to choose whether you operate from a place of judgment or a place of acceptance.

Deliberate Practice:

Step 1: Read the following questions out loud.

- » What's the problem?
- » Why can't I do this?
- » What are my limitations in making this change?
- » What's wrong?
- » Who's to blame? Whose fault is it?

Step 2: Write down how you feel after reading those questions out loud. Write down any adjectives that come to mind when you see and read those questions.

Step 3: Read the following questions out loud.

» How do I want to be different?

» What inner resources will support me in accomplishing this?

» How will making this change affect my life?

» When I make this change, how will I look and sound?

» When I make this change, how will I think differently?

» When I make this change, how will I move/act differently?

» When I make this change, how will I feel?

Step 4: Write down how you feel after reading the second set of questions out loud. Write down any adjectives that come to mind when you see and read those questions.

When reviewing the questions and adjectives you used to describe the questions in Step 1, you may have noticed being judgmental. Who were you pointing the finger at or were you harshly criticizing yourself? After reviewing the questions and adjectives you used to describe the questions in Step 3, you may have noticed a more expansive acceptance toward yourself. In these questions, there is a sense of curiosity and space for exploration.

You probably had a different visceral reaction to the questions in Step 1 compared to the questions in Step 3. In NLP, these questions are called the problem frame versus the outcome frame. Just like with the Judger and Learner mindset, you can choose empowering inner dialogue and questions to ask yourself. By simply changing your questions from a problem-frame to an outcome-frame, you will notice a shift in your inner dialogue.

When Mika shared the questions she was asking herself, they sounded like the following problem-framed questions:

Why did I leave financial services?
How will I prove myself as the only Asian on the team?
Will anyone listen to me when I have no tech experience?
What will my manager think about me?

When I asked her to shift her questions to an outcome-frame, we collectively came up with the following questions she could start asking herself:

How will I make the transition into the tech industry fun?
How will I use my Asian-ness to serve the team?
How can I leverage my twelve years of experience in financial services?
How can I ask my manager for what I need?

Bonus question: *What internal resources do I have that I can leverage when I start to speak negatively toward myself?*

When Mika started practicing pivoting from problem- to outcome-framed questions, she noticed considerable shifts in her inner dialogue, her perception of herself, and her mental well-being. When we are able to shift our perception of our skills and abilities, we are better able to speak up and advocate for ourselves. When you feel like an imposter, it's impossible to grab a bullhorn and ask for things such as a raise or a promotion. When you practice more compassionate, curious, and expansive questions, it helps you create a path of inner exploration where you are more likely to have the confidence to become your own cheerleader.

The questions we ask ourselves lead to our mindsets. From a Judger mindset, you are more closed-minded, certain, and critical. The focus is on problems rather than solutions and can often lead to defensive reactions, negativity, and stubbornness. In a Judger mindset, you look for differences and focus on right or wrong. The Judger mindset impedes progress by limiting perspectives.

In the Learner mindset, on the other hand, you are open-minded, curious, and creative. The focus is on progress, possibilities, leading to discoveries, understanding, and solutions. The Learner mindset facilitates progress by expanding options.[1]

Judger Mindset:	Learner Mindset:
Judgmental of self & others	Accepting of self & others
Inflexible & rigid	Flexible & adaptive
Self-righteous	Inquisitive
Defends assumptions	Questions assumptions
Personal perspective only	Open to perspective of others
More statements & opinions	More questions & curiosity
Possibilities seen as limited	Possibilities seen as unlimited
Primary disposition: Protective	Primary disposition: Curiosity

When in the Judger mindset, you are setting yourself up for a win/lose relationship with another person. When in the Learner mindset, you are setting yourself up for a win/win relationship.

Judger Relationship:	Learner Relationship:
Listens for right/wrong, agree/disagree, & differences	Listen for facts, understanding, & commonalities
Sense of being separate	Sense of being connected
Fears differences	Values differences
Feedback perceived as rejection	Feedback perceived as worthwhile

---

1   Marilee Adams Ph.D., *Change Your Questions, Change Your Life: 12 Powerful Tools for Leadership, Coaching, and Life* (Berrett-Koehler Publishers, 2016).

Criticizes	Critiques
Seeks to attack or defend	Seeks to resolve and create
Debates	Dialogues
Win-lose relationships	Win-win relationships

When in a Judger mindset, you are likely asking yourself problem-framed questions. If you are asking yourself problem-framed questions, chances are you are asking others on your team and internal/external collaborators the same types of questions. Because perception becomes reality, how would you like to be perceived? Would you like to be perceived as someone that debates, criticizes, and fears differences?

When in a Learner mindset, you are likely asking yourself and others outcome-framed questions. When you adopt a Learner mindset, you are perceived as someone that prefers a dialogue, is open to feedback, and seeks to resolve and create possibilities.

We all relate to both mindsets, and we have the power to choose which one in any given moment.

The choice is yours.

It's much easier to ask for a promotion or a raise when you are known as a collaborator and an open-minded facilitator of exploration, change, and progress. Inner exploration requires an expansive, curious set of questions, which then becomes your mode of operation. When you are operating from a Learner mindset, you mirror that open, curious energy with those around you. You become known for your curious, expansive mindset and well-respected for your work, which all leads to an effortless reach for the bullhorn of self-promotion.

Deliberate Practice:

Step 1: For the next week, I invite you to observe your inner dialogue. When the inner critic starts asking questions, identify which mindset you are operating from (Judger or Learner) and start to shift the questions to an outcome-frame instead of a problem-frame (just as I did with Mika).

Step 2: Once you get into the habit of identifying what frame you are in, shifting to more resourceful, outcome-framed questions will be easier to incorporate into your daily life.

The key to switching from Judger to Learner is awareness. From Dr. Adams, we can use the A-B-C-C Choice Process.[2]

A — *Aware*: "Am I in a Judger mindset?"

B — *Breathe*: "Do I need to step back, pause, and look at this situation more objectively?"

C — *Curiosity*: "Do I have all the facts? What else do I need to know?"

C — *Choose*: "What are my choices?"

Example: You receive unsolicited feedback from your manager about your most recent project.

You ask yourself a series of questions: "Why couldn't I get it right? What did I do wrong? Why am I not good at my job? When will I get it right the first time?" In some cases, the questioning can include cursing and calling yourself names.

---

2   Marilee Adams, *Change Your Questions, Change Your Life*, 85.

Aware: You feel a heaviness in your chest and know you are going into a downward spiral.

Breathe: You begin to practice a few rounds of deep breathing and return to the present moment.

Curiosity: You ask yourself, "What additional information do I need to get? Who can help me? What else do I need to know?"

Choose: You create choices for yourself. You can choose outcome-framed questions to help you create an action plan for next steps.

CHAPTER 8

INFLUENCING YOUR SELF-TALK

*"Watch what you tell your-
self, you're likely to believe it."*

—Russ Kyle

SABINA, AN AMERICAN-BORN BANGLADESHI MUSLIM,
worked in one of the top five consulting companies based in New
York City. Born and raised in Queens, Sabina was a devout Muslim
who prayed five times a day and wore a hijab—a religious veil cov-
ering her hair and head. In all of her schooling, she had no problem
sharing her background and explaining her lifestyle, but in professional settings, she felt intimated as she was the only hijab-wearing
Muslim woman in the office. When Sabina was promoted to manager, her responsibilities increased to include more client-facing
meetings and presentations.

When she was more junior in the organization, Sabina and I
worked on her communication skills and confidence levels pertain-
ing to her need to explain why she was excusing herself throughout the day to pray. She felt debilitating anxiety about communicating her needs to clients for fear of judgement, alienation, and
ridicule. Sabina kept saying, "I am not good at asking for what I

need." Like a broken record, she kept repeating this phrase. I asked her to add one minor addition to the statement: "I'm not good at asking for what I need YET!" A simple *yet* added the possibility that she could get better at asking for what she needs and that she is a work in progress. We opened each coaching session with this simple word as a self-compassionate gesture before we role-played conversations between her and a potential client.

I invite you to say the following statements out loud.

> Statement 1: I am not good at speaking up
> for myself.

> Statement 2: I'm not good at speaking up
> for myself YET.

Which statement feels better? Likely you chose the second sentence. The way we speak to ourselves impacts how we feel. We often spend the day in a continuous dialogue with ourselves. It may be about personal commentary, thoughts on life, judgments about yourself or others, or the circumstances of the workday. You have the ability to influence your thoughts with the words you choose. Adding a simple word like *yet* can alter the negative dialogue and create a shift in your physical and mental state.

As an underrepresented group in corporate America, there may be situations where you feel isolated, rejected, or misunderstood. In these instances, you may travel rapidly on a downward spiral of despair. Learning to influence your self-talk, as Sabina did, is a compassionate process to assist in handling those scenarios more resourcefully. When it comes to influencing self-talk, there are three phases to consider: Point It Out, Check It Out, and Work It Out.

PHASE 1: POINT IT OUT

This is when we become aware of our thoughts, feelings, and beliefs. Change begins with awareness. Because we spend so much time in autopilot, we don't notice our thoughts or internal dialogue unless we pause. With some deep breaths, we return to the present moment without catastrophizing about the future or ruminating about the past. Once we take a pause, we can step into the role of observer. Imagine you are in a movie theater watching a movie. You are an observer of the movie. When we are in observer mode, we can watch our words with distance and detachment. You can imagine the words landing in front of you, or perhaps you watch the words on the screen. In observer mode, you can shift into neutrality and notice your choice of words with curiosity versus judgment. After you have taken a few deep breaths and paused, becoming a neutral detached observer is crucial before moving to Check It Out.

PHASE 2: CHECK IT OUT

In this phase, the goal is to journey from a monologue to a dialogue with yourself. Imagine having a conversation with another person; you would never shush them or cut them off. (Well, hopefully not.) We give others respect by allowing them to finish their thoughts, and we owe the same courtesy to ourselves. Often, we don't allow ourselves to hear our thoughts for fear of what we may feel. In a rush to pacify any painful feelings and attempt to feel good immediately, we shush ourselves without fully listening. If we listened fully, what would our internal dialogue tell us? It might fall into one of three categories: Limiting ("I can't do this"), Positive ("I can do this"), and Possibility ("What if I can do this?"). When we shift from limiting self-talk to positive or possibility, it helps us be our own cheerleader.

Because no one will be a cheerleader for you, you must find ample opportunities to give a spontaneous self-salute for a job well done or provide words of encouragement when you are on the brink of creating something new. Most of us focus less on the positive or the possibility and give more energy to the negative self-talk. As such, when on a downward spiral of negativity, it's important to have strategies to challenge and disrupt the negative thoughts.

PHASE 3: WORK IT OUT

If you're on a downward trajectory of negative self-talk, Work It Out is the phase that provides strategies on choosing a more resourceful path. There are multiple possible strategies to use in this phase. Let's delve deeper on a five-part strategy:

Step 1: Pause & Breathe

Just like in Point It Out, the first step is to pause and breathe. In order to be more resourceful, we must return to the present moment. Taking a few deep breaths and pausing allows us to return from whatever downward spiral our mind's journey has taken to the present.

Step 2: Ask Challenger Questions

Question 1: Is this absolutely true?

Borrowed from Byron Katie's four questions from *The Work of Byron Katie*, the first question helps us truly reflect on the negative statement. For example, you might think *my manager dislikes me.* Ask yourself, is this absolutely true? Chances are, this is not a true statement. In the past, your manager asked you if you needed support or demonstrated her/his/their concern for you. When we ask ourselves "Is this absolutely true?" it's likely we can find evidence to prove that this negative self-talk is not a true statement.

Question 2: How is the opposite true?

Borrowed from Katie's *The Work*, the second question allows us to find evidence that disproves the negative self-talk. For example, if you think *my manager dislikes me*, ask yourself, "How is the opposite true?" The opposite of your manager disliking you is that she/he/they like you. When you ask yourself "Why does my manager like me?" your brain is thinking about the answer to that question. It can't contemplate anything else. Research in neuroscience has found that the human brain can only think about one idea at a time. When you ask yourself a question, you force your mind to consider only your question.

Question 3: Whose voice is it?

Is the voice of the negative self-talk yours? Disapproving relatives? Cultural norms personified via a critical parent? Societal norms personified through a critical friend? Is the voice a younger scared version of yourself? If so, refer to Pia Mellody's work, which I reference in Chapter 10 regarding taking care of the younger self. When we pause and identify whose voice we are hearing, it helps us move into an observer-detached position and decide what we want to do with this critical, disapproving voice. I've coached many Asian and South Asian women to find a phrase that works for them when they identify that the voice is not their own. Typically, the voice they hear is a critical, disapproving parental figure. Some phrases that have come up over the years are "Thanks for sharing, but no thanks" and "Thanks for sharing, but I can handle this." Developing and practicing go-to phrases help return your kind, compassionate, self-loving voice.

Step 3: Challenge the words you use: *always, never, have to, should*

Words like *always, never, no one,* and *everyone* are called universal qualifiers in NLP. These are generalizations that preclude exceptions or alternative choices. Consider, "I will never be good at speaking up for myself." A follow-up question to ask yourself would be, "Has there ever been a time when I did speak up for myself?" If you say to yourself, "No one at work likes me," a follow-up question might be, "When have you been liked?" Imagine there is a hockey goalie at the doorway of your mind. Allow them to block and question the absolute words and generalizations you use when speaking to yourself.

A simple shift from *have to* to *get to* can change your entire experience of a situation. "I have to deal with people talking over me in meetings" reframed to "I get to have another opportunity to learn to speak up for myself" changes your perception of the scenario and creates possibility rather than a perceived roadblock.

All day every day, are you telling yourself what you *should* do? We have been taught that if we don't should ourselves into action, we won't get anything done. *Should*-ing might have the opposite effect, where we feel so guilty, we may be paralyzed by inaction! The alternative is to use the word *just*. Instead of saying to yourself, "I should get this presentation done," consider "Once I finish *just* the first five slides, I will feel I have made progress." Once you move yourself into action, you'll notice that the five slides may turn into ten or twenty, and then eventually you complete the whole deck in one sitting. The goal is to just get moving because *just* is much more powerful than *should*.

Step 4: Ask yourself, "What may be the positive intention of the negative self-talk?"

In NLP, there is a presupposition that every behavior has a positive intention or purpose. Taking on this belief, even negative self-talk has positive intentions. A pattern I hear frequently with my clients is that they experience imposter syndrome and have negative internal self-dialogue around not being good enough to be in a position or organization. When it comes to imposter syndrome and negative self-talk, what might be the positive intention? The positive intention could possibly be that the negative self-talk is keeping you humble so you work harder. If we pause and take a few deep breaths, we can actually reflect and ask ourselves, "What is the positive intention of this self-talk that doesn't feel so great?"

When an organization chooses another vendor or a proposal doesn't get approved, I used to have this immediate reaction: *Oh no, Neelu, you are going to be homeless!* As crazy as this sounds, my mind would plummet in a downward spiral, quickly arriving to homelessness and poverty. Raised by two very hard-working immigrants, I inherited a fear-based relationship with money. The negative self-talk of becoming homeless was attempting to keep me safe. The internal chatter is actually trying to get me to press on the accelerator and keep moving forward with my business. This voice keeps me motivated! I have spent years working on my relationship with money and with this inner dialogue. The internal chatter is not as loud anymore, but I'm grateful when it shows up because it keeps me from swimming in a pool of complacency.

Step 5: Ask yourself, "What do I need in the moment?"

In Chapter 4, I mentioned Dr. Lisa Feldman Barrett's work from *How Emotions Are Made.* The concept of the body budget absolutely applies here. When in the midst of negative self-talk, are you sleep-deprived, hungry, or feeling depleted energetically? "What do I need in this moment?" is the question to ask yourself after pausing and taking a deep breath. Perhaps you need to eat a snack or take a power nap so the negative self-talk can shift to positive or possibility. The negative self-talk could be a direct result of your body budget being at a deficit.

When experiencing a deficit in your body budget, it's difficult to be your own cheerleader. For example, Alice had a performance review conversation scheduled with her manager while she was in the midst of moving homes during the COVID-19 pandemic.

She was dreading the meeting. She felt unprepared to speak up adequately for herself and she needed more time to get organized, but the deadline for the evaluations was approaching. Her self-talk was all negative, assuming the absolute worst-case scenario. She told herself she would not get a promotion and would be on put on a probationary period because she had been so distracted with the move.

When I asked her what she needed in the moment to have a productive conversation with her manager, her response was, "A long nap and an extra week to prepare." She knew exactly what she needed to do, but by simply hearing herself say the words out loud, she was able to take action. She explained her situation to her manager, and he agreed it made sense to wait a few days and have the conversation when she was better prepared. Had she forced herself to have a conversation she was unprepared to have, she would have been in an unresourceful state and would have not been able to properly advocate for herself.

Deliberate Practice:
Work It Out

Step 1: Think of reoccurring negative self-talk that occurs for you. Write it down in your journal or on a piece of paper.

Step 2: From the three challenger questions (Is this absolutely true? How is the opposite true? What do I need in this moment?), choose one to challenge your negative self-talk.

Step 3: Write down the response to the challenger question selected. Reflect on how you feel after you challenge your own negative self-talk.

Step 4: If you used words like *always, never, have to,* or *should,* what words can you choose instead? If you do not use these generalizations, skip Step 4.

Step 5: Write down the positive intention of this negative self-talk.

Step 6: Write down what you might need in the moment to pacify the negative self-talk. What might your body need in the moment?

Bonus: Work It Out with Play!

What if we could add a little joy and fun to the Work It Out phase?

Imagine for a moment that you can play and lessen the magnitude of your negative self-talk with a dial. Like the dial of a radio, you control how you want to play it. When we become playful, childlike, and make fun of ourselves, we can lessen the magnitude of the negativity.

The dial can include volume, location, tempo, rhythm, or tone. What would happen to the negative self-talk if you said it REALLY LOUD or if you whispered it softly to yourself?

What would the negative self-talk be like if you heard the voice near you or from a distance? What if the voice was above, below, or next to you? How might that change the impact of the self-talk?

What if you changed the tempo? What if you said your self-talk to yourself really fast? What if you slowed down the pace, as if in slow motion? How might that change the impact of the negative self-talk?

What if you adjusted the rhythm by singing to yourself? 𝄞 *I suck at my job. Oh...I suck at my job. Ohhhh, baby, I suck at my job!* 𝄞 How might singing your negative self-talk make you feel? Maybe you would laugh out loud. I use this one often because it often elicits a hearty belly laugh.

What if you used a constricted, tightly-wound tone with your self-talk? Or what if you shifted to a smooth baritone voice when speaking your negative self-talk out loud?

Deliberate Practice:
Work It Out with Play!

Step 1: Think of reoccurring negative self-talk that occurs for you. Write it down in your journal or on a piece of paper.

Step 2: Pick the dial you will play with: volume, location, tempo, rhythm, or tone.

Step 3: Say your negative self-talk using the dial you selected out loud.

Step 4: Repeat using a different dial until you laugh so hard your belly hurts.

CHAPTER 9

STEP INTO YOUR OASIS OF INNER RESOURCES

*"People have the inner resources to become any-
thing they want to be. Challenge becomes the
vehicle for tapping into those inner resources."*
—Erik Weihenmayer

IMAGINE FOR A MOMENT AN oasis of knowledge, wisdom, light, creativity, acceptance, wonder, harmony, and confidence. Guess what? This oasis is within you like a wellspring of resources that never runs dry. You have the ability to step into the resources you need in any given situation or circumstance. Because we are the only species that can travel through time with our minds, we can transport ourselves to the past or the future. We can retrieve information from the past or create new experiences in the future. All of the answers and resources are within us, and we can tap into this inner wellspring whenever needed using an NLP technique called Anchoring Our Inner Resources. Anchoring is a technique that creates a neurological connection between conscious behavior and an unconscious resourceful state that can be accessed at any time. Anchors can be visual (images), auditory (sounds or a mantra), or kinesthetic (touch).

Over the years, I have noticed a binary either/or pattern with the Asian and South Asian women I coached. Many of the women I have worked with had immigrant parents who pushed them to pursue more lucrative careers in math, science, engineering, or business for an immediate return on education investment versus social science, arts, or literature, where the paths after college or graduate school were less structured. Often the underlying belief is *I can either pursue what is expected of me or what I truly love to do, not both*. With this basic premise running in the background, there is a lack of confidence when pursuing a project, job, or career that doesn't fall into the culturally approved categories.

One of my clients struggled with this dilemma. Susie was born and raised in South Korea and migrated to the United States after graduate school. After twelve years working at a smaller software company, she decided she wanted to move to a larger, more well-known organization. Susie worked diligently and eventually become a senior software engineer at one of the largest tech firms based in the San Francisco Bay Area.

Susie quickly climbed the corporate ladder as she became the go-to person on her team for anything related to finding code errors. She was masterful in the role of code auditor, but she struggled immensely with public speaking. If someone asked her a question in a team meeting, she would be able to quickly articulate her thoughts, but if asked the same exact question in a larger group, she would become paralyzed with fear, sweat profusely, and couldn't stop stuttering. I wouldn't have believed she was so nervous had she not shown me videos of her presenting at her company's townhall.

Susie believed she could either be good at hard technical skills or soft communication skills; she couldn't excel in both. She believed her Asian educational roots revered technical skills and mocked interpersonal communication skills. "What if you could be both an excellent software engineer and an excellent public speaker," I asked her in one of our coaching sessions. With a look of disbelief, she stated that she was trained as an engineer, not as a communication specialist. The either/or pattern inhibited her from considering that it was even possible for her to develop a soft skill. Using her metaphor of hard versus soft skills, I began coaching Susie in public speaking and divided our sessions into two categories: hard, tactical public speaking techniques and soft, reading-the-room-and-responding-accordingly skills. This method resonated well with Susie, and she was able to grasp the concepts rather quickly, improving her public speaking skills drastically.

Alongside public speaking coaching, I helped Susie access her inner resource of confidence with the NLP anchoring technique. We used a previous situation when she felt confident and created a kinesthetic anchor that she could embody before any public speaking engagement. Anchoring confidence when public speaking was a game changer for Susie. She began pursuing high-visibility initiatives and now had two pom poms in her hands: technical code auditor and public speaker extraordinaire. Susie didn't need a bullhorn to be her own cheerleader because her technical and communication skills led her to numerous promotions.

Anchoring has also helped me greatly in my career. When I am teaching, speaking in front of a large audience, or coaching one-on-one, I need different sets of resources. Through the anchoring techniques of NLP, I can step into the resource I need in any given situation. For the sake of simplicity, we will create a kinesthetic anchor using touch.

Imagine you are about to deliver a high-stakes presentation to a mixed audience of coworkers, managers, cross-functional partners, and the partner of the division. The inner resource that you may need in the moment is confidence—confidence to present with ease, to deliver an engaging message, and to handle questions and answers tactfully.

We are going to access your inner oasis of confidence; however, the anchoring process can work with any inner resource you want to access.

Deliberate Practice:

Step 1: As you begin to gently close your eyes, take a deep breath in and balloon the belly out. As you exhale, bring the belly in toward the spine almost as if you are giving yourself a hug with the abdomen.

Step 2: In a calm, relaxed state, think about a time when you experienced confidence. It can be a time in your past when you were feeling confident. Take a deep breath, relax, and let the memory come to mind in which you felt confident.

Step 3: See what you see, hear what you hear, and feel what you feel as you experience confidence. You can take all the time you need to experience confidence throughout your whole body, fully and completely.

Step 4: Choose an anchor that involves touch, such as touching your thumb and index finger together or making a fist. Be creative. Find an anchor that is unique and easy for you to remember.

Step 5: Remember what you saw, heard, and felt when you experienced confidence. Put yourself inside the memory as if you are reliving it. Do not view the memory from a distance. You've got to actually be there again.

Step 6: Relive the memory of confidence until you begin to feel the confidence coming over you in the same way you felt it at that time. As you feel the confidence, fire off your anchor from Step 3.

Example: Touch your thumb and index finger as the feeling of confidence increases. Release the thumb and index finger when the feelings begin to subside.

Step 7: It's time to test the anchor. Gently begin to close your eyes and apply your anchor (Example: thumb and index finger touch) in exactly the same way again. See if you are able to easily access confidence. If it worked, congratulations! You now have an NLP anchor of confidence and can access it any time to feel confident. (Note: You can repeat this process with any other inner resource you need to access, just remember to choose different anchors.)

If this anchor technique did not work, repeat steps 1 to 5 and try again.

CHAPTER 10

BE IN TIME OR THROUGH TIME— THE CHOICE IS YOURS

"There is nothing permanent except change."

—Heraclitus

HAVE YOU EVER WONDERED WHAT happened to a big chunk of time in your life? I can't remember large chunks of my childhood and adulthood. However, there are certain moments that I have cherished in the past and can easily access. They are etched in my memory, and when I was experiencing them, I wanted the moment to last forever, like when I graduated from Columbia University with my master's degree. I can remember how I felt in that very moment, wishing it would never end. I was truly *in* the moment.

Conversely, there are moments in time where I felt so stuck and didn't know if they would ever end. An immediate example that comes to mind is the six weeks in October 2018 when I was in a boot after fracturing a bone in my right foot. My mom came and stayed with me to take care of me, and I was confined to my apartment, unable to do very much. I literally felt like the time would never end. I waited, counting the hours and days until my next podiatrist appointment. I was so in the moment I thought it would never end.

In NLP, there is a concept referred to being *In Time*. When you are in time, it feels like the time will last forever. You have no access to other feelings from other times and places. As you can see from my examples, you can be in time during a beautiful moment and enjoy it blissfully, or you can be stuck in time during a not-so-beautiful moment. The choice is absolutely yours. You can revel in the moment, or you can be in a stuck state for a lot of moments.

The alternative to being stuck in the moment is a concept called *Through Time*. Through time is when you feel that there is a sense of change, movement, and continuity between past, present, and future. Sometimes, when we are experiencing something perceived as terrible, it's really helpful to remind ourselves that there is nothing permanent except change, as Heraclitus, the Greek philosopher so eloquently said. Time is fluid, constantly moving, and things never stay the same. This is really helpful to remember when experiencing something that feels like it will never end.

These concepts made a big difference for a client named Ateefa. Pakistani-born and American-raised, she was a senior financial analyst who worked for a large investment bank based in New York City. I met Ateefa when I was facilitating Present with Confidence, a public speaking communication class based on executive presence. She approached me after class and asked me specific questions related to difficult conversations with her manager. We started working together in a coaching relationship soon thereafter.

When we began our one-on-one sessions, she shared scenarios where she had a very difficult time asking for what she needed, whether it be leaving work early to pick up her children from school, responding to feedback she received, or asking for a promotion. Before any one-on-one scheduled conversation with her manager, she began feeling anxiety and dread. She worked herself up so much before the conversation that by the time the meeting occurred, she had already spent extensive amounts of time suffering, feeling uneasiness and discomfort in advance.

Then, when the meeting started, she thought it would never end. She described the meetings as a movie playing in slow motion. Ateefa was very much *In Time* in her meetings with her manager. I asked her what it would be like to think of her meetings as fluid, constantly moving and changing—a moment in time that would pass. We worked through techniques that allowed her to reframe her thoughts to be *Through Time* as she prepared and had the one-on-one meetings with her manager. Whether you are in a similar situation as Ateefa or you find yourself in a different, uncomfortable scenario where speaking up or advocating for yourself feels like time is moving at snail speed, the concept of *In Time* versus *Through Time* provides a flexible tool to compassionately massage the illusion of time for your mental well-being.

The concepts of *In Time* and *Through Time* were illuminated for me in 2010 when I was working for a very large financial services company. It was my first job after completing my master's degree. I was excited to put all of the information I learned to use and had an intense desire to teach and coach. During a performance review and bonus reveal conversation, my manager slid a piece of paper face down toward me. The paper would reveal the whopping bonus that I had earned for all of my heart-filled, passionate work over the year. You probably won't believe that when I turned the paper over, the amount was zero. Apparently, the company wasn't doing as well as expected, and my manager shared that our division was not given funds to allocate. I literally felt like time stood still. The image of turning over that piece of paper is etched in my memory forever.

I left the room feeling unmotivated and sick to my stomach, wishing I was not in that situation. This feeling lingered until there was a massive downsizing and I was let go three years later. In hindsight, I'm so grateful that door closed because many others opened up that brought me closer to fulfilling my purpose. Looking back at the situation, the advice I would give to my younger self would be to remember that nothing is constant. There is always movement *In Time*, and absolutely nothing stays the same. If I knew about the concept of *Through Time* back then, it would have saved me a lot of heartache because I felt stuck for far too long. When you find yourself in a difficult situation, it's helpful to have an anchor of *Through Time* as a gentle reminder that this too shall pass.

Deliberate Practice:

Step 1: Take a moment, and gently close your eyes. Focus on inhaling and exhaling as you begin to feel connected to your center. Continue focusing on your breath until you feel grounded, calm, and fully relaxed.

Step 2: Think of a mantra that resonates with you to gently remind you that this feeling or time shall pass.

Step 3: Continue to say this mantra or auditory anchor silently to yourself. Check in with yourself and ask, "Does this mantra sound like me? Is this something I would say to myself? Is this something that will help me snap out of a stuck state?" If so, move to step 4. If not, find another mantra that resonates with you.

Step 4: Think of a time where you felt like time was standing still. Really allow yourself to be in the experience. Hear what you hear, feel what you feel, and see what you see as you experience feeling stuck as if time were standing still.

Step 5: Silently say your mantra while in that memory. Continue to say it and see how the outcome might have been different.

Step 6: Revisit the mantra you have chosen. In your journal, write down other mantras or phrases that would be gentle reminders that this too shall pass.

Time is our most finite resource. As we reflect on moments in time that consumed our precious energy, we might wonder *why did I waste so much time and energy on that situation?* The choice of being *In Time* or *Through Time* is yours. The more you practice using your *Through Time* mantras, the less likely you are to exert wasted energy and precious time ruminating over a past scenario. I hope the concept of *Through Time* is as helpful to you as it was for me and Ateefa.

CHAPTER 11

WHO'S REALLY IN CHARGE?

"Holding on is believing that there's a past;
letting go is knowing that there's a future."
—Daphne Rose Kingma

"I STEPPED INTO THE CONFERENCE room, hands shaking, voice quivering with utter and complete fear that I was going to bomb the meeting I was expected to lead with the senior executive team. I had been preparing for weeks, and this was a pivotal moment. I finalized the proposal and was about to present my findings to the team. The senior executive team then presented the proposal to a multimillion-dollar client. All of the hours of research, incorporating multiple inputs and finalizing the deck, seemed to be coming to a head in this very moment. All I could think of was, 'What if I screwed up collecting all the pieces of information, or what if I come across as incompetent?'"

This was one of the situations that Kim, one of my coaching clients, described to me as she told me about the vortex of stress she was experiencing. As she described the situation, her hands were shaking and her voice was quivering, almost as if she were experiencing the same reaction while she described the situation to me.

I asked Kim, "Who was in charge when you walked into the conference room?"

She looked at me with a blank stare. Then, she responded, "What do you mean who was in charge. I was in charge."

Really? Was thirty-three-year-old Kim in charge? Or was it the fourteen-year-old who was terrified she was incompetent? I bring up fourteen-year-old Kim because in the past she told me she had some developmental blockages. Her parents had divorced, and her teenage mind couldn't wrap itself around the perceived damage to her family. As a single child of Chinese immigrants, her parents' divorce shook her to her core, and she spent a couple of years experiencing mental anguish, guilt, and fear. She fell behind in school, and her grades slipped substantially. By the time the dust settled a bit, she was sixteen and spent the next year and a half trying to catch up her failed grades. Kim felt incompetent and paralyzed with fear about her future. She was letting the younger, scared, fourteen-year-old part run the thirty-three-year-old adult show.

Pia Mellody, an internationally renowned lecturer on the childhood origins of emotional dysfunction, has researched and written about how we often ask the small child (children) in us to handle adult situations. There may be emotional traumas during our childhood that are so painful that we can't seem to get past them, or we regress to different ages where we are emotionally stunted in our growth to adulthood. In *Breaking Free*, Mellody identifies indications that you have put a child in charge of a particular situation.

Indications you have put a child in charge: (From Mellody in *Breaking Free*)

1. You are overwhelmed. The adult feelings are TOO BIG for this little part of you to handle. It's the feeling of having all of your tasks seem as if they are run-on sentences with no punctuation. When you are in this state of being overwhelmed, you are unable to put a comma between all of the run-on sentences engulfing your mind.

2. You are feeling or acting in extremes. You might use words like *always* and *never*. An example would be saying, "Things never work out for me. Why does this always happen to me?"

3. You have no boundaries. You are taking everything personally. For example, you call a friend and don't hear back. If you are in your small child self, you start imagining that your friend doesn't like you anymore and think it is not fair that they do not like you, or you begin wondering what you've done to make them angry. Over the next few days when your friend reaches out to you, you learn that their phone died, and they never received your voicemail. Instead of thinking about what could have possibly been going on with your friend, you take the experience as if it's personal to you, doubting and judging yourself.

4. You are reacting to triggers rather than responding resourcefully. You have no ability to pause, breathe, and choose a more resourceful response. For example, if someone says something upsetting, you become defensive and respond immediately without pausing and thinking through a more appropriate response.

5. Reality is intolerable, so you have to medicate or numb out your feelings by drinking, drugs, sex, romance, work, being busy, or whatever is your preferred method of numbing yourself. For example, you are miserable at your job, and the way you cope is excessive shopping to numb the pain of being unfulfilled at work.

6. You are lying or hiding your honest thoughts and feelings. You are trying to adapt to make someone else feel comfortable to protect yourself. For example, you are unable to share your true feelings with a friend to protect yourself from possible rejection.

7. You have rules that apply only to you. Examples include:

    a. You are very understanding when someone else feels or does something, but you are very self-judgmental and self-critical when you do it yourself.

    b. You understand that other people are not perfect, but you judge your own imperfection very harshly.

    c. It's fine if other people share their vulnerabilities or mistakes, but you have a rule that you must seem (at least on the outside) perfect.

        These rules are the result of the coping mechanism from childhood of trying to be perfect, so you can survive and not make someone angry.

8. Your reactions are out of proportion. For example, you have one disagreement with your manager, and your day is ruined because you are convinced that you are going to get fired.

If you experience any of the eight indications mentioned above, according to Mellody, you are putting a child in charge of an adult situation. We've all been there and likely can recall times when we have had childlike responses to situations. Self-awareness is the first step, but what do we do when we are in the moment, triggered and having a childlike reaction?

Mellody suggests a process to put the adult back in charge. How would you be with a real child of this age who was having these feelings?

Here is the process of putting an adult back in charge:

1. Ask yourself how old is this little part of you? Is it a baby? Is it a three-, five-, or thirteen-year-old? I often regress to the age of fifteen, when I felt like I had no voice, was unable to leave my parent's home, and was dealing with a variety of emotional and physical abuse. Thirty-three-year-old Kim was letting her insecure fourteen-year-old self run the meeting.

2. Bring to mind what you were like at that age. After you have identified the age of the younger version of you, see your younger self sitting in front of you. What is she wearing? How does she look? What is the expression on her face? Notice what you notice about this child in front of you.

3. Identify what the child part is feeling. What emotion is she feeling? Happy, sad, angry, scared, or ashamed? When you ask her how she is feeling, what does she say? Speak to her. Ask her how she is doing.

4. What does she need? To be listened to? To be held? What does she need to hear from you? What can you tell her that will help her in the moment? This is not about lying and pretending things are different. This is an honest conversation between the adult and the smaller, younger part of you.

5. Apologize to the child for putting her in an adult situation. Let her know (in a language she can understand) that it's not her job to handle your adult life. Remind

her that she is safe and that you are capable of taking care of things and keeping her safe. What will you tell her to assure her that she is safe? What can you tell her about what's to come later in her life that might make her feel safe as a fourteen-year-old?

6. Imagine a place the child would love to be at and an adult caretaker she would love to be with. The caretaker can be a real person (grandma, auntie, uncle), living or dead, a fictional character, or a spiritual being (Buddha, an angel, or God). I used to have a best friend in middle school who had two sisters. I loved going to their Italian home because they were so joyous and inclusive. Her mom was our caretaker (RIP Trudi Fiscarelli) while we all played, and I felt so safe. Reflect for yourself. Where would this younger part feel safe and with whom?

7. In your mind's eye, put the child and the caretaker in the safe and fun place. Allow the child to feel safe and protected, so the adult is back in charge and can run the show.

It's difficult to be a cheerleader for yourself when there is a scared, younger part attempting to take over. A small child who reaches for the bullhorn might scream gibberish or an illogical fear-based argument. It takes an adult to grab the microphoned bullhorn, speak up to ensure you get credit where credit is due, and communicate your contributions authentically. Let's practice Pia Mellody's work of identifying when the child is taking over and how to put the adult back in charge.

Deliberate Practice:

Step 1: Close your eyes and take a deep breath. Feel your feet grounded to the earth. As you inhale, balloon the belly out, and as you exhale, bring the belly in toward the abdomen as if you are giving yourself a hug. As you continue to breathe, reflect on a time in the recent past when you felt one of the eight indications that you were putting your inner child in charge of an adult situation. What was the situation? Write it down in your journal.

Step 2: Move through the steps identified in putting the adult back in charge mentioned above.

Step 3: Ask yourself, "How would I have responded or behaved differently had I put my adult self forward?" Write down any key reflections of how you would have handled the situation differently if the adult was in charge.

Step 4: Remind yourself that once you get into the habit of identifying times when the adult-you was not in charge, it becomes easier to pinpoint the age of the younger part of you that is trying to take over. You can then take care of the child and allow the adult to run the show. Remember that practice makes permanent. Once you make this a habit, you can move through the steps of putting the adult in charge quickly. This is not meant to be a long process that takes hours. You can literally move through the steps in a few quick minutes prior to a situation where you need the adult you to fully be in charge.

CHAPTER 12

AS IF...

"As a single footstep will not make a path on the earth, so a single thought will not make a pathway in the mind. To make a deep physical path, we walk again and again. To make a deep mental path, we must think over and over the kind of thoughts we wish to dominate our lives."
—Wilferd Arlan Peterson

THROUGH OUR THOUGHTS, WE CAN experience pure bliss or suffer immensely. It seems simple, right? Change your thoughts, and you can change how you feel. Essentially, yes, but sometimes when we are feeling stuck, our thoughts take a downward spiral, and it's challenging to step out of the bottomless pit of despair. You may be a in a job that isn't satisfying or in a role that is not serving you, but the good news is that your thoughts can ultimately change situations and desired outcomes. I worked closely with Karima to challenge her thoughts.

Karima, a Malaysian-born, American-raised lawyer, migrated to the United States with her family at the age of thirteen. She felt awkward in her brown skin, didn't speak English very well, and carried feelings of non-belonging in all social settings, particularly in her Caucasian-dominant schools. She never felt that she fit in and only had two friends in high school. Karima believed the only reason the two friends hung out with her was because they were all lumped into the "other" category.

Her family landed in Pittsburgh in a neighborhood that was not diverse. She was one of the very few people of color in her entire school. Karima would tell herself she was not attractive because she witnessed Caucasian girls getting all of the attention. She struggled with depression and anxiety throughout her childhood and adult life. Karima was very intelligent and immersed herself in her schoolwork with the hopes that education would be her ticket out of her painful life. She graduated with honors from high school, college, and an Ivy League law school.

Karima was a successful senior real estate attorney at a law firm based in Philadelphia. Goal-oriented, determined, and driven were some of the adjectives she used to describe herself. If she wasn't working toward a goal, the negative self-talk returned, and she would go through serious bouts of depression and anxiety, resulting in imposter syndrome and feelings of inadequacy about her career despite everything she had achieved. When she was overwhelmed, she became apathetic and sluggish. Karima felt she couldn't function and found herself taking multiple leaves of absence from work for weeks at a time. Because I had worked with Karima for over five years, I recognized the best way for her to get out of her own way was to work backward and have her create action items in digestible chunks of time using the As-If Frame.

Through spiritual studies, I learned about the vibrational effects of speaking and writing as if events already occurred. In the spiritual realm, it's associated with visualizations and affirmations, which I will discuss in the spiritual section of the book. From an NLP and psychological perspective, the As-if Frame is a powerful tool.

The As-If Frame allows you to tap into your subconscious and ask, "What do I truly desire?" It involves a reorientation of time by stepping into a future state. As you establish what you want to accomplish in a given time, it also allows you to identify skills, knowledge, and desired outcomes that you want to experience in the future. When you participate in a scenario as if it has already occurred, you change your internal state and learn steps leading up to achieving future outcomes.

Karima and I used the As-If Frame every quarter to reflect inward, so she could identify and communicate her professional desires. The As-If Frame was powerful for Karima because once she vocalized her true desires, we could work backward to create an action plan. The hardest part was to truly reflect on her desired outcome(s) and release the fear of failure. I would guide her into a deeply relaxed state, and we would travel through time, landing in a future date where she would tell me all she had accomplished. I would ask her questions about what she did to achieve the goal(s). In the As-If Frame, you speak as if scenarios have already occurred, so you use the past tense. For example, we worked together a few months ago, and the date was January 1, 2021. During that session, we traveled through time to April 1, 2021. We worked together to identify what she had accomplished by that future date and what steps she took to achieve these bite-sized, digestible, three-month goals.

Because Karima would get overwhelmed if we forecasted too far in advance, we played around with the duration of time that felt comfortable for her, which was three months. You can use the As-If Frame for six-month, one- , five- , or even in ten-year increments if you want to focus on longer-term goals. Karima was determined to be promoted to partner at her law firm in the next three years, so we created bite-sized, digestible, quarterly chunks of goals that would lead up to a promotion. Some of those goals were to be chosen to represent the firm in high-profile engagements, identify who she needed to speak to, and how and when she would grab the bullhorn and advocate for herself internally and externally with clients. As we identified what needed to occur, we co-created a specific action plan in three-month increments.

Sometimes when we daydream, we think our desires are far-fetched. We tend to overestimate what we can accomplish in a day and underestimate what we can accomplish in a month. Imagine having a road map for your desired goals that leads you down the path of fulfilling your true desires. Professional success must be married to self-promotion. Being your own cheerleader includes communicating your accomplishments and identifying the people who need to be informed of your success. The As-If Frame is an effective tool that allows you to create a deliberate plan of action, incorporating what to do and who needs to know what you are doing.

Deliberate Practice:

You'll need your journal or paper to write.

Step 1: As you sit in a quiet, safe place, think about the areas in your professional life that you would like to change. (Example: get a promotion, change roles, find a new job, switch careers, etc.) In your journal, write down these areas as categories on the top of the page.

Step 2: As you sit still with your feet firmly planted on the ground (or cross-legged if that is more comfortable), spine tall but not rigid, begin to breathe in (balloon the belly out) and breathe out (belly in toward the spine). Begin to slow the breath down. Begin to slow the thoughts. Begin to gently close your eyes.

Step 3: You can relax your jaw and let your tongue rest in the pool of your lower mouth.

Step 4: Visualize yourself in a time travel capsule or machine, traveling through time into the future. With each inhale and exhale, you move through seconds, minutes, days, weeks, months, and maybe even years depending on the timeframe that feels comfortable to you.

Step 5: As you gently open your eyes, imagine is it one year from the actual date. For example, if it is January 1, 2022, imagine it is January 1, 2023. (Remember: If one year feels too long, adjust the increment of time that feels comfortable to you.)

Step 6: Remaining in the As-If Frame, speak about what you have accomplished in the present tense in first person. (Think of the categories you identified in Step 1.) For example, if you wish to change your job, you might say, "I now have my dream job as VP of sales" or "I asked my manager for the promotion I deserve." It doesn't matter if you are practicing this alone or in a group, it is important that you speak out loud. Speak as if you have already accomplished what you desire.

Step 7: After you have identified and spoken the desired outcomes out loud, write them down in your journal.

Step 8: Remaining in the As-If Frame, ask yourself the following questions and write down anything that comes up for you.

What are you thinking?
How are you feeling?

How are you acting differently?

What steps did you take months earlier to achieve this outcome?

Who did you reach out to for support?

Who needs to be informed of all you have accomplished?

Step 9: Focus specifically on the question *What steps did you take months earlier to achieve this outcome?* Write down any and all things that come to mind. Do not second-guess what comes to mind; simply write it down.

Step 10: Begin to gently and slowly close your eyes. With feet grounded to the earth, imagine entering into your time travel capsule or machine. With every inhale and exhale, you find yourself moving through years, months, weeks, days, minutes, and seconds arriving back to today in the present moment.

Step 11: As you open your eyes, you are in the here and now. Look at your journal and notice if there are small actionable steps that you can start immediately. You can now put a plan together that will help you achieve your desired goal(s).

Gentle reminder: You have all the answers. The As-If Frame helps to tap into the knowledge within.

Step 12: Create a plan of action for yourself with milestone dates to hold yourself accountable. If you have a hard time holding yourself accountable, communicate your intentions to an accountability partner or coach.

CHAPTER 13

FLEXING THE RESILIENCE MUSCLE

*"The man who moves a mountain begins
by carrying away small stones."*

—Confucius

RESILIENCE IS DEFINED AS THE capacity to overcome diffi-
culties. Resilience is often used to describe how individuals make
it through big life challenges, such as illness, divorce, or losing a
job. Yes, resilience most certainly applies to those life-altering situations where we learn about ourselves and our character, perhaps
defined as macro-level resilience.

There is also something I like to refer to as micro-level resilience. This is resilience that we have and may not even be aware
of. For example, you come home after a long day of work, open
your mailbox, and see an unexpected, very high medical bill. We
all have our own process of dealing with difficult situations, but at
some point, you investigate, analyze, and attempt to refute it, but
if it's accurate, you pay it and move on. The key is that you move
on. It might have taken you one day, three days, or one week, but
eventually you moved on.

Although getting an unexpected medical bill is a completely different context than losing your job or going through a divorce, it still involves resilience; it's either macro- or micro-level resilience, but it's resilience nonetheless. The more challenges you power through (big or small), the more you build the resilience muscle. We tend to forget we have this muscle because we don't take a step back and think of micro-level resilience—it's often labeled as everyday life.

I helped Aditi uncover the micro- and macro-resilience muscles that she had forgotten. Aditi, born in a household of two parents from India, was raised in Hong Kong. Her parents migrated to Hong Kong when Aditi was three years old. Culturally, Aditi considered herself a Hong Konger, but outwardly, she looked Indian. She felt that looking South Asian was eventually going to become an obstacle in her career, so she decided that at some point she wanted to move to the United States.

Aditi was working as a senior manager at one of the top five consulting companies based in Hong Kong. After her divorce, she decided to move to the United States to start a new chapter and attempt to be promoted to partner in the New York City office. Aditi convinced a few partners in the Hong Kong office to agree to the transfer and found an ally in the New York City office who would take a chance on her in a completely different sector of the company.

Aditi and I met at a networking event in New York City, and she hired me as an executive coach soon thereafter. After a few months of working in the New York City office, she called me on a Friday afternoon and left an urgent voicemail saying she needed to speak to me immediately. When I called her back, she told me she wanted to leave her job and start her own business. She was terrified, unsure of herself, and doubting her abilities.

We met a few days later, and she explained that she came from a long lineage of business owners. The desire had always existed, but she kept putting it off because she was climbing the ranks in the consulting world. Being in New York sparked her entrepreneurial spirit, and she wanted to take a plunge into unknown waters. She wanted to create an exclusive, high-end, catering business, but she wasn't sure how her work in the corporate world would translate. *Can I make such a big leap? Will people hire me? Will they trust my company to feed loved ones during momentous occasions?* These were just some of the rapid-fire questions that were pouring out of her in one of our sessions.

"Aditi, did you take a huge leap unto unknown waters when you decided to get divorced? What were the steps you took that led you to make such a big decision to move to the United States? What steps did you take to convince partners in Hong Kong to sign off on your transfer?" These were just some of my follow-up questions to her questions. Like Aditi, we often reflect back and think of the big life-altering experiences and lose sight of the micro-level resilient moments we endured to move through large obstacles. Having gone through a divorce myself, I often reflect back and think of the wellspring of macro-level resilience I tapped into, but I forget about the daily, bite-sized, chunks of resilience I leveraged to get back on my feet.

I worked with Aditi to identify chains of macro-resilient events, where each link represented a micro-resilient action. The chains we worked on were divorce, transferring to the United States, working her way up the corporate ladder to senior manager, and starting a new business. Each session was dedicated to identifying all of the links in the chain, so Aditi became aware of her resilience muscles. This process allowed Aditi to become her own cheerleader and acknowledge herself for all of the courageous micro-level resilient actions she took to move through great obstacles and achieve massive goals.

To be your own cheerleader, it takes awareness, reflection, and acknowledgment of all the macro- and micro-level resilient muscles you have flexed. As you consider the big chains in your life, let's take a moment to reflect on all of the links that worked together to create the chain.

Deliberate Practice:

You'll need your journal or paper to write.

Step 1: Close your eyes and take a deep breath. Feel your feet grounded to the earth. As you inhale, balloon the belly out, and as you exhale, bring the belly in toward the abdomen as if you are giving yourself a hug. As you continue to breathe, reflect on a big challenge you've gone through in your life or a huge achievement you've accomplished. Notice what you notice as you bring this memory to mind.

Step 2: As you begin to open your eyes, draw a chain that has many links on your paper. The chain represents a big challenge or huge achievement you've accomplished. Give your chain a name. (Example: divorce, career switch, promotion, etc.) You don't have to draw a perfect chain. Draw anything that resembles a chain.

Step 3: As you look at the links of the chain, think about all of the courageous micro-steps or actions you took. Write down each step on each link of the chain on your paper.

Step 4: As you review the links of the chain with loving kindness toward yourself, acknowledge all of the times you flexed the micro-level resilience muscles.

If you are having difficulty giving yourself a pat on the back, imagine this is your best friend's chain, and you are telling her how proud you are of her for getting through such a huge challenge or for achieving such a massive goal. When it's comfortable, you can move from third person to first person speaking about yourself.

Step 5: For a moment or two, allow yourself to feel proud of yourself. Imagine for a moment an audience filled with younger versions of you cheering for all of the small steps you took to move forward.

Part III
Connecting to Your Center

"The place you are right now,
God circled on a map for you."

– Hafiz

CHAPTER 14

PRACTICING INACTION

"The body benefits from movement and
the mind benefits from stillness."
—Sakyong Mipham

IN YOGA PHILOSOPHY, THERE ARE *yamas* (social restraints)
and *niyamas* (self-disciplines). These are ethical principles that provide a recipe for living in the world with ease. Within the *niyamas*,
one of the principles is called *saucha* or purity. *Saucha* refers to the
purification of the body, thoughts, and words. In our culture, we
have an implicit social contract that we will not leave our home and
enter society without showering, brushing our teeth, and cleaning
our external body. Just as we clean our physical body, a cleaning of
our mind needs to occur before we enter into the world.

Imagine walking out of your home with so much mind chatter
that you arrive at the subway or bus stop without realizing how
you got there. Or, even more frighteningly, you end up at work
after driving for an hour on autopilot. This can happen because
we spend at least 95 percent of the day in unconscious thoughts.
We are often unaware of our thoughts, words, and actions. Just as
showering or brushing our teeth is something that is considered
basic hygiene practices, we have a social contract to not leave our
home in haste or with anxiety. That haste or anxiety can impact

every interaction we have with every person or being we encounter. Not only can it impact our interactions with others, but it also most certainly impacts our internal dialogue. Mental hygiene or internal purification can be achieved through meditation.

Reverend Michael Beckwith from the Agape Center in Los Angeles describes meditation as paying undistractable attention to reality. It is a habitual practice of training the mind to focus and redirect thoughts. Meditation can be used to increase awareness of yourself and your surroundings. If we think of external cleaning as a social contract before we leave our homes every morning, we must think of meditation as an internal shower that is equally important and essential every day.

You might wonder, how does meditation relate to self-promotion? We hear the term "monkey mind" for a reason. Our minds can be unsettled, restless, capricious, whimsical, fanciful, confused, indecisive, or uncontrollable. When there is extensive internal mind chatter, it's challenging to think logically, feel resourceful, and communicate coherently. Imagine speaking up for yourself and pulling out the bullhorn for self-advocation while feeling tongue-tied with a distracted mind. When the mind is full of stuff, meditation clears out the noise and makes space for clarity and articulate communication.

Imagine that you receive feedback from your manager and adamantly disagree. Throughout your entire commute home, you are reliving the conversation. You are analyzing each and every word. Finally, you arrive home. You mindlessly eat dinner and can't stop thinking about the conversation. In bed, you are distressed and have disturbed sleep. You wake up thinking of the feedback. The conversation you had yesterday has you on a one-way route to the land of rumination. Rumination is defined as the process of continuously thinking about the same thought.

One of my clients, Jessica, suffered from debilitating ruminations about her previous job where she was downsized. The ruminations of the past were prohibiting her from moving forward in
her new job and role. Jessica, born and raised in Vietnam, worked
as a successful senior product manager at a large tech firm based in
the San Francisco Bay Area, and suffered from chronic crippling
anxiety. When something would go awry, whether it was a difficult
conversation with her manager or a disgruntled team member, her
mind raced in a downward spiral of severe doom, reliving trauma
from her past employer.

Her past employer had multiple rounds of layoffs over the
course of three years, but she seemed to hang on until the very end.
Jessica would go to work every day, feeling her stomach in knots
and thinking she could lose her livelihood and her ability to live
and work in the United States at any minute. She was eating lunch
at her desk, rushing to complete a presentation when she received
a phone call from her manager asking her to come to the conference room in one hour. She made her way to the conference room,
her heart racing, short of breath, tightness in her chest and tears
rolling down her face. Jessica was close to attaining a green card,
and if she was let go from her job, she would have to find another
organization that would sponsor her and restart the lengthy process. As expected, she was let go and escorted out of the building
within the hour.

Jessica couldn't find another organization to hire and sponsor
her in the allotted time, so she was forced to return to Vietnam.
It took her two years to return to the United States, and she said
they were the hardest two years of her life. She used up all of her
savings and was struggling emotionally and financially. The downsizing, losing her green card status, and the financial instability
were traumatic events that she ruminated about every time there
were challenges in her current role. Days before every performance

review conversation, Jessica would be paralyzed with fear and could not control the downward spiral of negative thoughts and crippling anxiety.

Even though she was fully prepared to have the conversation with ample data points for a well-deserved promotion, she couldn't move past the trauma stored in her body. I worked with Jessica to clear the negative chatter and cleanse her mind, using mediation as an internal shower to let go of her past trauma associated with losing her job.

If you have issues with ruminating thoughts, meditation can be a healthy distraction. I know the word *healthy* is quite subjective. In this reference, I'm suggesting the opposite of unhealthy, which might be junk food, alcohol, drugs, or binging on Netflix or YouTube. The ruminations can cease by simply bringing awareness to your breath. When we meditate, we return to the present moment. When we ruminate, we are typically living in the past or catastrophizing about the future. If focusing on your breath is not so easy for you, you can try a mantra (a word or sound that aids in concentration) that resonates with you. This mantra can come from your spiritual or religious practices. Often, breath with mantra can be combined. A very simple mantra to use with your breath is "let go." On the inhale, silently say "let," and on the exhale silently say "go." This is a mantra that can help you return to the present moment.

I teach meditation to groups and individuals, and the most common thing I hear is that people don't have time to sit still for twenty minutes or one hour. In Zen Buddhism, there is a quote that applies specifically to the excuse that there is not enough time to meditate: "Meditate for an hour every day unless you are too busy. In that case, meditate for two hours." If you don't have time, feel rushed, or are overwhelmed, you likely need to meditate for more than five minutes, but if that's all the time you have, then that will just have to work! The idea is to be non-attached to the outcome of the duration of your daily meditation.

Some of you will say, "If I don't have twenty minutes, I won't sit still at all." The inner shower happens no matter how long you sit. Sit still for however long you have time to sit still without being attached to the number of minutes or hours. You will enter your day in a calm, balanced state. Once it becomes a habit, you will notice how differently you feel when you don't meditate every morning. We are our worst critics and will be tempted to judge ourselves if we don't sit for a number of minutes daily. The goal is to remain unattached to the amount of time that you can meditate. Simply attach yourself to the daily practice of meditation despite the length of time. Practice makes progress, and when meditation becomes a daily habit, it can be an easily accessed tool in moments where the mind chatter is loud and consuming.

Deliberate Practice:

Try this first thing in the morning after you wake up.

Step 1: Sit in a comfortable, cross-legged position on a cushion, or if you are in a chair, feel your feet firmly grounded to the floor. Feel your spine, tall but not rigid. Feel one straight strong line of energy from the crown of your head to your tailbone and from your tailbone to the crown of your head.

Step 2: When you feel ready, begin to gently close your eyes.

Step 3: You can relax your jaw and let the tongue rest in the pool of your lower mouth.

Step 4: Bring your attention and your focus to the inhale. As you inhale, balloon the belly out. As you exhale, bring your belly toward the spine as if you are giving yourself a hug with the abdomen.

Step 5: Inhale, balloon the belly out. Exhale, belly in toward the spine.

Step 6: Continue with your deep, long, abdominal breaths. As you inhale, silently say "let," and as you exhale, silently say "go."

Step 7: When the mind wanders, gently and lovingly return the mind to the inhale and the exhale.

Step 8: Continue sitting, breathing, and focusing on your breath for as long as you like.

Step 9: When you feel complete, begin to gently and slowly open your eyes.

Step 10: Taking all the time you need, begin to reorient yourself to your surroundings.

Step 11: Take this feeling of calm and balance with you as you enter the day, and use this as a tool to control the mind chatter.

Reminder: This feeling of peace and serenity is available to you at all times during the day through your breath. You don't have to sit on a cushion or seat to return to this place of peace.

CHAPTER 15

ATTACHMENT, NONATTACHMENT, OR DETACHMENT. HOW ATTACHED ARE YOU?

"Attachment is the source of all suffering."
—Buddha

HAVE YOU EVER WANTED SOMETHING so bad that you were clinging on for dear life? You couldn't stop thinking about this thing you wanted: a promotion at work, a person you wanted to be with, or a situation you desperately felt you needed to be involved in. In Buddhist philosophy, attachment is seen as a narrowing of perception that makes you unable to see limitless possibility. When we are attached, we are consumed with our limited expectation of a desired outcome.

Detachment means to distance oneself from the world because of disinterest. Detachment can be seen as a sense of aloofness that separates oneself from the rest of the world. When we are detached, we are distant and disconnected from self and others.

Nonattachment is a practice of presence and mindfulness. You are fully committed to the task, situation, or relationship, but you are not attached to an outcome. Buddhism describes nonattachment as being in the world but not of the world. When you practice nonattachment, your happiness is no longer defined by anything outside of you.

When we are practicing nonattachment, we are not clinging to ideas, revelations, things, people, jobs, or relationships. We have awareness of them, but there is a sense of ease and flow. The type of nonattachment that Buddhism speaks of is not about what you want, but how you hold on. The need to hold on so tight is related to impermanence. Suffering occurs because we continue to hold on to a person, thing, or experience past the expiration date. Heraclitus, the Greek philosopher said, "There is nothing permanent except change." Because things are constantly changing, when we attach or hold on so tight, suffering is inevitable.

Nonattachment sounds wonderful in theory, but how do we practice it when we live in a society of constant seeking and attainment? I am not suggesting that you eliminate goals and milestones in your life or career. I am suggesting that you let go of the reins and stop identifying so strongly with job titles, goals, or experiences. As it relates to being your own cheerleader, nonattachment can take many forms. The energy used to grasp so tightly can be used in more impactful ways.

In 2013, prior to being downsized, I was anxiously anticipating a promotion. After meeting all of the criteria and continuously working on my internal personal brand, there was really nothing more I could do. I couldn't control the promotion process, but what I could control was my attachment to the result. After I put all the wheels in motion toward a promotion, the energy exerted on obsessing could have been used to work on a whole host of other personal or professional pursuits. When it comes to self-promotion and self-advocating, taking action toward the desired goal is necessary, but letting go of the result is equally crucial for the sake of your mental well-being.

One of my spiritual teachers once suggested to avoid punctuating the end of my goal. She said, "No need to add a period or exclamation point. The goal doesn't need to end. Keep going." At the time, I wasn't quite sure what she meant by keep going, but over the years, the way I interpreted that statement was to create the goal, work toward the goal, and instead of ending the goal with a period or exclamation point, add a comma. The comma, depending on your spiritual beliefs, could be surrendering to God, the Universe, or a higher power.

The comma can elicit fear because it is unknown territory. How do you add a comma at the end of a goal and hold space for the uncertainty of the unknown? There is no better time to figure this out than now. As I write this chapter, we are experiencing the global pandemic of COVID-19. In this moment, many of us have lost clients, work, and jobs. Uncertainty is the only guarantee. As each day passes during the quarantine, we must practice nonattachment to our pre-pandemic life. We must practice nonattachment to whatever arises after the comma. This is the time for all of us to practice holding the space for the uncertainty of the unknown and befriending our fear.

Fear was the predominant emotion for Priya during the COVID-19 pandemic. She was the primary breadwinner, and she lost her job. She experienced a lot of fear about the uncertainty of when she would find another job that paid a comparable salary to her previous job. Priya and I worked together years ago, and she reached out during the pandemic, hoping I could help her cope with her anxiety, self-promote during her job search, and communicate with influence in her upcoming interviews. She had been at her previous job for a decade and felt that her interviewing skills needed to be sharpened. Fear and anxiety were impacting her confidence and her ability to clearly articulate her value.

Fear is an emotion that many of us fear. We don't know what to do with it, so we are scared to feel it. I worked closely with Priya to help ramp up her interview skills, deal with her anxiety, and prepare for the upcoming interviews. We discussed grabbing the bullhorn and highlighting the initiatives from her previous role that would showcase her experience and value. These were all tactical things that we needed to address, but they would fall short if she didn't befriend her fear.

I asked her to think about the state of the world and how each and every one of us is experiencing fear of the unknown. When I helped her see that she wasn't the only one in the same situation, she began to let go of the reins of control. She was prepared to do her best on the interviews because that was something she could control. Priya couldn't control the outcome of the interviews. When we are in a state of nonattachment, we are mindful of the moment, and we do the best we can do. Then we let go of the outcome after the moment is over. This can only occur if we address and became acquainted with the fear of the unknown.

In her book *When Things Fall Apart*, Pema Chödrön suggests we must become intimate with our fear. Borrowed from the Tonglen practice of Buddhism, she encourages moving close to the fear and just being there with it. By encountering and befriending fear, you cannot be paralyzed by it. Fear that arises in the moment increases the capacity to encounter what is alive in the present moment. Connecting with fear involves compassion with ourselves and with our fear.

Maybe you have lost your job, gotten a new job, switched roles, or started your own business during the COVID-19 pandemic. In any of the situations mentioned, you may experience fear as it relates to self-promotion. If you do experience fear, you are not alone. It's not an easy reach for the bullhorn to self-advocate when there is so much uncertainty about what the future of work looks like.

We are certainly in the midst of so much collective societal and individual fear. Sometimes the fear can be debilitating as we have no idea what tomorrow holds. Our health, finances, and social structures are being challenged in a way we have never experienced before. I invite you to practice entering into your fear and letting go of the reins of control with Pema Chödrön's meditation.

Deliberate Practice: Placing the Fearful Mind in the Cradle of Loving Kindness

Reminder: There is nothing to figure out. Going into the body and getting in touch with the feeling of fear with the breath will allow you to breathe into the restricted tight areas. The wisdom of the body knows how to heal itself. Leave it up to the body to heal and allow this meditation to alleviate patterns of rumination and anxiety.

Step 1: Sit in a comfortable, cross-legged position on a cushion, or if you are in a chair, feel your feet firmly grounded to the floor. Feel your spine, tall but not rigid. Feel one straight strong line of energy from the crown of your head to your tailbone and from your tailbone to the crown of your head.

Step 2: When you feel ready, begin to gently close your eyes.

Step 3: You can relax your jaw and let the tongue rest in the pool of your lower mouth.

Step 4: Bring your attention and focus to your breath. As you inhale, balloon the belly out. As you exhale, bring your belly toward the spine as if you are giving yourself a hug with the abdomen.

Step 5: Inhale, balloon the belly out. Exhale, belly in toward the spine.

Step 6: As you begin to breathe deeply, feel your mind and thoughts slowing down. When you have a thought, let it go. Be an observer of the thought(s). Let them gently come in and gently go out with the inhale and exhale.

Step 7: As you breathe, notice where the fear resides in your body. Where in the body is there constriction or a feeling of tightness/clinging? Are you holding fear in your jaw, shoulders, solar plexus, heart, or shoulders? Where is the constriction in the body?

Step 8: Breathe deeply into the location(s) of the body where you are feeling fear.

Step 9: On the next inhale, feel the fear physically without thinking about it. On the next exhale, take a big, deep, long, relaxing exhale.

Step 10: On the next inhale, breathe in a sense of opening and warmth, and on the exhale, breathe out with a sense of opening and warmth.

Step 11: Continue breathing expansive, compassionate, loving, warm breaths in and out. There is nothing to figure out. There is nothing to solve or do. Simply be with the breaths that are warm and open. Move through the unresourceful, stuck, fearful state with the breath.

CHAPTER 16

EVERYTHING IS OPERATING FOR YOU

"Vision without action is fantasy.
Action without vision is chaos."
—Dr. Michael Beckwith

YOUR MIND DOESN'T KNOW THE difference between imagination and reality. Your thoughts are energy vibrations that can have a powerful influence on the way you experience reality. As Henry Ford said, "Whether you think you can or think you can't, you're right." Visualizations, affirmations, and afformations (a concept by Noah St. John) can train your subconscious into adopting new beliefs. By activating the creative subconscious, you can seek solutions and shape your desired reality.

Visualization is the process of creating a mental image with your mind's eye. Visualizations help prepare your brain to recognize and receive the resources you'll need to reach your desired outcome. When we visualize a goal as already complete, the creative subconscious is activated, providing access to pathways and ideas that will help reach your goal. When the vibrations of our thoughts are operating at a higher frequency, the law of attraction suggests that positive experiences are drawn to us.

After I applied to graduate school, I spent a few minutes every morning visualizing myself opening my mailbox, touching the letter, opening the envelope, reading "Congratulations, you've been accepted!," jumping up and down, squealing with joy, and getting on the elevator of my apartment building. I focused on each and every detail and engaged all five senses in the visualization. In case you are wondering, when I received my acceptance letter to Columbia University, I did follow through on each of the actions in the visualization. Visualizations are powerful tools to train your brain to operate at a higher frequency. Athletes use visualization to program the brain to reach the desired outcome, and so can you.

If you are less visual and more auditorily inclined, affirmations can be used to influence your subconscious mind to access new beliefs. Affirmations are positive statements declaring a specific goal in their completed state and can become daily mantras that have a profound effect on reprograming the subconscious mind to create the reality you want. They can serve as inspiration or simple reminders. Affirmations can also serve to focus attention on goals throughout the day, which has the potential to promote positive sustained change.

One of the simple affirmations I use daily that helps me get through difficult situations is, "I can handle anything that comes my way." Anytime I receive any form of rejection, whether from a potential client or a publisher, I repeat, "I can handle anything that comes my way." I repeat this phrase as a mantra throughout the day to help create positive sustained change. Another affirmation that I repeat as a mantra is, "There is no such thing as failure, only feedback." This reframe has helped me compassionately receive constructive feedback. What is a simple affirmation that would be easy for you to remember and repeat?

Sometimes an affirmation may fall flat because your logical mind is challenged with believing statements that you perceive as false. An example I run into frequently is somepne having a phobia of public speaking. If you use the daily affirmation, "I am an amazing public speaker," and you don't believe that to be true, the affirmation will not resonate. You may take a plunge into a pit of despair because you believe you will never be a good public speaker, and the brain will provide more reasons and data why you are not a good public speaker. The solution? Afformations.

The Book of Afformations by Noah St. John defines afformations as empowering questions that immediately change your subconscious thought patterns from negative to positive. When you ask a question, your mind automatically begins to search for an answer. In psychological terms, it is referred to as the embedded presupposition factor. If you ask yourself why you are such an amazing public speaker, your brain will start searching for an answer. When we ask ourselves empowering questions, our brains focus on finding the answer, and we will attract what we focus on. This is also known as the spiritual law of attraction. As Dr. Michael Beckwith says, "Energy flows where attention goes." The law of attraction tells us that like attracts like, and to have the things we desire, we must vibrate at a higher positive frequency.

When it comes to afformations related to self-promotion, confidence, and career, there are a few that I consistently use and encourage my clients to experiment with:

Why do I have the courage to do what I love and ask for the money I'm worth?

Why am I so good at my job?

Why is it so easy for me to speak up for myself?

Why does success come so effortlessly?

Why are my talents expressed and appreciated at work?

Let's bring our attention and focus to vibrating on a higher frequency using visualizations, affirmations, and afformations.

Deliberate Practice:
Raising Our Vibrational Frequency

Scenario: Imagine you are advocating for a promotion. You will be speaking to your manager to discuss all of your accomplishments and influence her to be an advocate for you at the roundtable discussions on your behalf. This is the moment in time when it is critical for you to fully articulate all of your efforts and hard work during the past year. You have prepared and finalized your inputs in the performance review document that you will be reviewing with her, but you still feel a ball of nerves in your stomach before the meeting. What will you choose to focus on? How will you raise your vibrational frequency to match your level of preparedness for this big moment?

Visualization:

Step 1: Sit comfortably in your chair with your feet grounded to the floor. Feel your spine tall but not rigid. Feel one straight, strong line of energy from the crown of your head to your tailbone and from your tailbone to the crown of your head.

Step 2: When you feel ready, begin to gently close your eyes.

Step 3: You can relax your jaw and let the tongue rest in the pool of your lower mouth.

Step 4: Bring your attention and focus to the inhale. As you inhale, balloon the belly out. As you exhale, bring your belly toward the spine as if you are giving yourself a hug with the abdomen.

Step 5: Inhale, balloon the belly out. Exhale, belly in toward the spine.

Step 6: Visualize the end of the meeting. Either you are walking out of the room or you are closing the Zoom screen (if virtual). You are standing or sitting tall. You have a smile on your face. You feel that you did a great job articulating everything to set your manager up for success and to be your advocate at the roundtables. Notice what you are seeing, hearing, and feeling. Take a moment, and breathe in the images, sounds, and feelings as you experience an epic success.

Affirmations:

Perhaps you have been using daily affirmations from the moment you started preparing for the performance review conversation, or maybe you decide to spend the morning before the meeting affirming your desired outcomes. Your affirmations may sound like:

I can advocate for myself.
I am so good at my job.
I nailed the meeting. (Use the past tense as if the event already occurred.)
I am valued at this company.

Notice how you feel. Perhaps these affirmations worked. What if you are still having a hard time believing that you can easily advocate for yourself? You can experiment with afformations.

Afformations:

Remember that when you ask a question, your brain automatically starts searching for an answer. What if your afformations sounded like the following?

Why is it so easy for me to advocate for myself?
Why am I so good at my job?
Why did that meeting go so smoothly?
Why am I such a valued employee at the company?

Reflection:

Notice how you feel. What is the embodied difference between the affirmations and afformations? Notice any sensations in the body.

Per Noah St. John, afformations start with *why* and not *how*. The *why* is your motive for doing something and the *how* is the method. We know this from much research about the power of the *why*. The motive drives action, and the *how* is simply the mechanics. We will figure out the *how*, but we will only take action when we know the *why*. You afform, "Why is it so easy for me to speak up and advocate for myself?" Your mind immediately seeks the answer to the question and forces you to think of all the reasons that it is easy for you to self-promote and advocate for yourself, which increases your vibrational frequency. Refer to *The Book of Afformations* for afformations on career success, abundance, love, and intimacy among others.

Added Bonus:

Dr. Beckwith suggests adding animated emotion to your afformations. Perhaps you can stomp your foot and shout, "Why am I such a powerful advocate for myself?" Not only will it elicit a smile, but you are continuously amplifying your vibrational frequency. The universe will match this frequency and operate for you.

Whether you use visualizations, affirmations, afformations, or all of the above, you will begin to train your subconscious into adopting new resourceful beliefs. Before we can grab the bullhorn to speak up and be our own cheerleader, we must let go of disempowering beliefs about our abilities and our self-worth. We can only communicate our value when we believe we are valuable. To retrain your brain, I invite you to experiment with visualizations, affirmations, and afformations.

CHAPTER 17

AWARENESS AND CLARITY WITH THE FIVE GREAT ELEMENTS

"What is necessary to change a person is
to change his awareness of himself."
—Abraham Maslow

AYURVEDA IS KNOWN AS THE science of life. It is a holistic healing system of medicine based in India. Five thousand years ago, Ayurveda evolved in the meditative minds of seekers of truth, rishis. For thousands of years, their teachings were transmitted orally from teacher to disciple and later documented in melodious Sanskrit poetry. Though many of these texts have been lost over time, an abundant body of Ayurvedic knowledge survives.

According to an excerpt from Dr. Vasant Lad's *Ayurveda: The Science of Self-Healing: A Practical Guide*:

> Originating in Cosmic Consciousness, this wisdom was intuitively received in the hearts of rishis. They perceived that consciousness was energy manifested into five great elements (Mahabhutas):

Ether (Space), Air (Vayu), Fire (Agni), Water (Jal), and Earth (Prithvi). This concept of the five elements lies at the heart of Ayurvedic Science. From the state of unified consciousness, the subtle vibrations of the cosmic soundless sound AUM manifested. From that vibration, first appeared the Ether (Space) element. This ethereal element then began to move; its subtle movements created the Air, which is Ether in Action. The movement of Ether produced friction, and through that friction, heat was generated. Particles of heat-energy combined to form intense light and from this light the Fire element manifested. Thus, Ether manifested into Air, and it was the same Ether that further manifested to Fire. Through the heat of the fire, certain ethereal elements dissolved and liquified, manifesting the water element, and then solidified to form the molecules of Earth. In this way, Ether manifested into the four elements of Air, Fire, Water, & Earth.

Ayurveda believes we are a microcosm of the macrocosm. As such, these five great elements (*Mahabhutas*) are found in nature and within each cell of our being. With awareness of these elements in our daily life and interactions, we have opportunities to leverage the wisdom of the elements and respond resourcefully when facing challenging situations. Knowledge and awareness of the five great elements can help us illuminate our true nature, allowing us to tap into the internal wellspring of resilience we all need to cultivate when we are advocating for ourselves. When the elements are balanced internally, it's much easier to grab the bullhorn and speak our truth.

#1–2 OF THE GREAT ELEMENTS—ETHER (AKA SPACE) & AIR

The Ether element is clear, light, subtle, immeasurable, expansive, free, and formless. The Air element is lightness, motion, breath, and oxygen; it's like wind (the movement of ether). We associate the air in our body with the air we breathe. The rishis recognized this Air as the immediate source of life, also referred to as prana (life energy).

When in a difficult conversation with someone, wouldn't it be helpful to have more spaciousness and movement? Space brings freedom to respond more resourcefully, and movement brings a lack of rigidity and the ability to breathe deeply. Often, we think we are right, and the other person is wrong. What if we could allow for some movement from our constricted view to open ourselves up to the other person's perspective? We can start by pausing and taking a few deep breaths. Creating spaciousness helped Hana receive developmental feedback.

Hana and Rani were once colleagues and friends at work. When Rani got promoted, Hana reported directly to her. This new power dynamic challenged both their friendship and professional relationship. They had to have mid- and end-of-year performance review conversations where Rani delivered constructive feedback that was upsetting to Hana. Rani told Hana that she lacked confidence and did not have executive presence in meetings. When Hana heard this feedback, she was angry, hurt, and disappointed. When I asked Hana how she felt in her body when she received the feedback, she said she felt constricted with heat arising in her belly and tightness in her shoulders. I guided her to a practice of cultivating more spaciousness and movement in her body with the following practice from Wendy Palmer's work in *Leadership Embodiment*, combining practices from Aikido and mindfulness.

Step 1: As you inhale, lengthen and lift up through the crown of your head. As you exhale, soften and think of someone or some being that makes you smile.

Step 2: Imagine yourself in a sphere, a spacious sphere, that is inclusive of yourself and the other person/being.

Step 3: Think of the criticism and the specific words used. Allow the words to land in the spacious sphere in front of you. Look at the words from a distance. The criticism has landed in the space, not in your body.

Step 4: As you look at the words from a distance, notice if you have a different sense of the criticism. Notice if you are able to take the feedback less personally as you observe it from afar.

Step 5: Ask yourself, "Is there any validity or anything useful in this feedback?"

When I led Hana through this centering and spacious exercise, she realized she wanted to work on her executive presence. She realized that she took the criticism personally because her friend, now manager, was delivering the feedback to her. When we can create spaciousness and move out of our triggered emotions, we will have a more resourceful response. If self-advocacy looks like asking for a promotion or speaking up for your work, spaciousness in your mindset can create room for well-formed, clearly-articulated, communication. Movement and mobility of the Air element brings the ability to sway from a fixed mindset to a flexible and expansive one.

Deliberate Practice:
Creating Space and Movement in Receiving
Developmental Feedback

Step 1: Think about any criticism you have received.

Step 2: After a moment or two, allow it to land in your body. Identify how it feels in the body. Where are you experiencing any sensations in the body? What is the temperature (if any)? Write it down in your journal.

Step 3: Shake it out. Let it go.

Step 4: Let's begin Wendy Palmer's Centered Listening Exercise:

» As you inhale, lengthen and uplift through the crown of your head. As you exhale, soften and think of someone or some being that makes you smile.

» Imagine yourself in a sphere, a spacious sphere, that is inclusive of yourself and the other person.

» Think of the criticism and specific words used. Allow the words to land in the spacious sphere in front of you. Look at the words from a distance. The criticism has landed in the space, not in your body.

» As you look at the words from a distance, notice if you have a different sense of the criticism. Notice if you are able to take the feedback less personally as you observe it from afar.

» Ask yourself, "Is there any validity or anything useful in this feedback?"

Step 5: Notice the difference between your initial response to the criticism versus when you went through the Centered Listening Exercise.

#3 OF THE GREAT ELEMENTS—FIRE

Ether provides fire the space to burn while Air provides fire the capacity to burn. The third element, Fire, evolves from Ether and Air. The sun is the generator of energy for the earth, and fire is the generator of energy for the body. The Fire element is hot, sharp, bright, upward moving, and spreading. The Fire element brings intelligence and an ability to cut through the surface appearance of things, along with the capacity to transform information to reach deep understanding.

When harnessed and channeled appropriately, the Fire element can help when you have trouble speaking up or voicing your opinion. Fire is paradoxical in nature; it can be harnessed to speak up and sustain life, but on the other hand, it can destroy everything on its path. We want to harness this fire energy responsibly. Channeling the Fire element helped Lily speak up for herself.

Lily, a mid-level manager in financial services, was born and raised in China and came to the United States for a job. I started coaching her two years after she arrived in the United States. Lily had an accent when she spoke English and felt unsure of what words to use in meetings when she wanted to speak up. She mentioned that when she was about to speak in meetings, she felt a gnawing, aching pain in her abdomen. When I asked her what the color of the pain was, she said, "bright red." I asked her if we could turn the bright red into a yellow healing color like the sun. The sun as a nurturing energy could help her focus, harness her drive and ambition, and speak up when she needed to through *Interruption Shield phrases* (refer to chapter 5).

Interruption Shield phrases are phrases that can be used when you want to interject in the middle of a meeting or a conversation when it seems there is no space for your voice. As a woman of color, I have found a few go-to phrases that have worked for me over the years: "If I may...," "May I....," "Can we pause here...," or "I would like to interject here..." Speaking up in meetings caused Lily much anxiety, so we worked through a visualization of soothing the Fire element. We created and practiced Interruption Shield phrases that allowed her to move into a stretch versus panic zone.

Deliberate Practice:
Harnessing the Fire Element to Speak Up

Step 1: Take a deep breath. As you inhale, lengthen the spine. As you exhale, bring your belly toward the spine as if you are giving yourself a hug with your abdomen. As you begin to deepen the breath, visualize this yellow, healing, solar energy in your solar plexus like a candle flame—steady and constant.

Step 2: Think of Interruption Shield phrases that you feel comfortable with. Write down the ones that come to your mind.

Step 3: Practice makes progress. Use your phrases whenever you can. Using Interruption Shield phrases to help you speak up for yourself is like building a muscle. When you become more comfortable speaking up and voicing your opinions in everyday meetings, it will be much easier to grab the bullhorn in high-stakes conversations like performance reviews. If you do not advocate for yourself, no one will.

#4 OF THE GREAT ELEMENTS—WATER

The Water element is cool, stable, heavy, moist, smooth, flowing, dull, cloudy, and soft.

Water is the principle of cohesion. In the body, this emerges as nourishment, growth, and lubrication. It is important to take in the qualities of Water when you are feeling too warm, ungrounded, emaciated, dehydrated, rough, lacking in self-esteem, obstructed, immobile, irritable with a sharp tongue, transparent, vulnerable, or if your heart has become too hard.[1] When you express clarified Water element, you feel nourished by and connected to your community. It helps you feel content and express yourself calmly and smoothly, allowing things to roll off your back.[2]

Water is a transformative substance. When it runs over any other element, it changes it forever. The way in which the Water element transpires at work is in an attitude of togetherness and camaraderie. What would it be like to have an attitude of *we are all in this together* when dealing with a difficult team or individual at work? We would assume the other person has a positive intention, and in that moment, they are doing the best they can. We can cultivate this sense of togetherness and access the Water element when we find a common denominator with the person/people with whom we are having a challenging conversation. The calming effect of the Water element helped Sandra, a senior manager in a large consulting company, deal with a challenging situation.

Sandra was feeling bullied in her new role. The other members of the senior leadership team were trying to convince her to do something she fundamentally disagreed with. The bullying was

---

[1] Dr. Marc Halpern, California College of Ayurveda (blog), "The Five Elements: Water in Ayurveda," June 10, 2010, https://www.ayurvedacollege.com/blog/five-elements-water-ayurveda/.

[2] Susan Fauman, Banyan Botanicals (blog), "Exploring the Elements—Water," November 11, 2016, https://www.banyanbotanicals.com/info/blog-the-banyan-insight/details/exploring-the-elementswater/.

in the form of covert threats about being moved to a different division or potentially losing her job if she didn't agree with the rest of the team. She was very angry, frantically going down the path of name-calling, and I interrupted her to ask, "What would it be like to pour water over your anger? What would be like to have water wash over your anger right now?" I asked her to take a moment to let the Water element wash over the anger and to take a deep breath.

As she calmed and settled down, I asked her, "Why do you think the other members are saying these things to you?" With some reflection, she responded that they were also fearful of losing their jobs. The common denominator is fear, which is the emotion associated with the Water element. The Water element allows soothing of temperament and the ability to relate to those around us.

Deliberate Practice:
Accessing the Water Element to Experience Togetherness

Step 1: Take a deep breath. As you inhale, lengthen the spine. As you exhale, bring your belly toward the spine as if you are giving yourself a hug with your abdomen. As you begin to deepen the breath, take a moment to fully pause your racing mind.

Step 2: Think of an individual/group of people at work that is eliciting frustration or anger. Write down the words that are coming to mind about this person/people.

Step 3: Visualize pouring water over the words. Visualize pouring water over the anger you are experiencing. What happens when you pour water over flames?

Step 4: Ask yourself, "Why might this person be behaving this way?" Write down your answer.

Step 5: Notice if you have a different perspective on this individual/group of people. Write down how you feel differently about the person/people.

#5 OF THE GREAT ELEMENTS—EARTH

The Earth element expresses as stability. The qualities of the Earth element are cool, stable, heavy, dry, rough, gross, dense, dull, and hard. When you express clarified Earth element, you feel stable and rooted. Emotionally, you are grounded, confident, and flexible. You make well-considered decisions, and you don't doubt yourself in carrying them out. The Earth element supports committed, long-term relationships and career paths.[3]

How might the Earth element help when you are feeling frazzled and overwhelmed at work? When our minds are racing and our thoughts are scattered, a grounding, calming energy is required to balance the Air and Space elements. The Earth element provides a sense of connection and grounding that is helpful when we are stressed and feeling overworked.

Pre-pandemic, I used to travel at least once a week to facilitate workshops across North America. For over a year now, the travel has ceased, yet I am working longer hours than ever before. Because the commute to the client has been temporary eliminated, I find myself in back-to-back Zoom meetings, feeling overworked and needing to play catch-up on all of my tasks that have been ignored because of the meetings.

---

3   Susan Fauman, Banyan Botanicals (blog), "Exploring the Elements—Earth," October 27, 2016, https://www.banyanbotanicals.com/info/blog-the-banyan-insight/details/exploring-the-elements-earth/.

As I continue to work with teams and individuals across industries virtually, I know I am not the only one experiencing the need to play catch-up throughout the day. Many have moved to different locations to ride out the pandemic. There is a sense of uncertainty eminent for all of us, particularly as it relates to job security. Many individuals I coach are questioning if they are on the verge of a lay-off, given the economic devastation that has occurred this past year. You may be nervous to ask your manager for what you need, because of the fear of losing your job. With uncertainty comes catastrophizing future possible scenarios.

Whether you feel overwhelmed because of the increased daily workload or you feel anxious to speak up regarding your personal needs due to fear of losing your job, the Earth element can provide a sense of stability and heaviness that is resourceful when the mind is racing and scattered.

Deliberate Practice:
Accessing the Earth Element to Feel Grounded During Stressful Times

Step 1: Take a deep breath. As you inhale, lengthen the spine. As you exhale, bring your belly toward the spine as if you are giving yourself a hug with your abdomen. As you begin to deepen the breath, allow the mind to relax. Allow the thoughts to slow down.

Step 2: As you continue to breathe deeply through the abdomen, feel your feet grounded to the earth. If your legs are crossed, begin to uncross them. As you ground your feet into the earth, spread your toes out as wide as you can. Press into the balls and heels of the feet, and feel the support of the earth beneath you. Allow your hands to rest facing down on your lap.

Step 3: Feel the support of the surface beneath you. It could be the seat of the chair, the support of the floor, or the grass beneath you if you are sitting outside. Feel the support of whatever surface is beneath you, and feel the surface connect to the earth.

Step 4: For just a moment, give thanks and appreciation to Mother Earth for providing you structure and support. You can access this support through your feet at any time—no matter where you are seated or standing. You can access this feeling of calm steadiness at any time through your breath and feet.

BONUS Step 5: If available to you, ground your feet to the earth while barefoot in grass. Also, known as earthing, you can access a calm mind, better sleep, and reduced pain by grounding your feet barefoot into the earth.

For more information on grabbing the bullhorn through the self-care practices of Ayurveda, see Appendix III.

CHAPTER 18

ACCESS YOUR POWERHOUSES

"Each of the seven chakras are governed by spiritual laws, principles of consciousness that we can use to cultivate greater harmony, happiness, and well-being in our lives and in the world."
—Deepak Chopra

IN SANSKRIT, THE WORD CHAKRA translates to a wheel or disk. In yoga, meditation, and Ayurveda, this term refers to wheels of energy throughout the body. There are seven main chakras aligning along the spine, beginning at the base of the spine and tracking all the way up to the crown of the head. Because chakras are subtle fields of energy, you cannot see them through an X-ray, but you can visualize them as swirling wheels of energy associated with different colors and sounds.

The first three chakras are more physical in nature and focused on basic survival.

The first chakra (*Muladhara* in Sanskrit) addresses our sense of stability, security, and basic needs. When this chakra is open, we feel safe and fearless. This also relates to our physiological needs from Maslow's Hierarchy of Needs. The first chakra is located at the base of the spine.

The second chakra (*Svadhisthana* in Sanskrit) addresses our creativity and is our sexual center. It is responsible for our creative expression. The second chakra is located a few inches above the base close to the pelvic area.

The third chakra (*Manipura* in Sanskrit) literally translates to *lustrous gem* and is our source of personal power. This energy center houses our motivation, ambition, and drive to succeed. The third chakra is located at the navel.

The fourth chakra connects the first three to the last three.

The fourth chakra (*Anahata* in Sanskrit) is at the middle of the seven and unites the lower three chakras to the upper chakras. The fourth serves as the bridge between our body, mind, emotions, and spirit. It is considered the heart chakra, and it is our source of love and connection to ourselves and to others.

The last three chakras are more spiritual in nature.

The fifth chakra (*Vishuddha* in Sanskrit) is our source of verbal expression and the ability to speak our truth. It is associated with communication. When this chakra is open, we are able to communicate our highest truth. When blocked, it could contribute to the inability speak to others, establish boundaries, and live in harmony with ourselves. The fifth chakra is located near the throat.

The sixth chakra (*Ajna* in Sanskrit) is commonly referred to our third eye. It is the home of our intuition and is located between the eyebrows.

The seventh chakra (*Sahasrara* in Sanskrit) is known as the thousand petal lotus and is responsible for our spiritual connection to our higher selves, others, and our divine creator. This chakra is located at the crown of the head.

To be in a healthy balanced state, all chakras need to be aligned. For the purposes of self-promotion and self-advocacy, we will bring attention and focus on harmonizing the third and fifth chakras. To be your own cheerleader, you must tap into the powerhouse of the third chakra and communicate your value clearly and articulately, which is available when the fifth chakra is aligned.

The third chakra is also referred to as the solar plexus. It provides a source of personal power and relates to self-esteem, warrior energy, and the power of transformation. Associated with the Fire (*agni*) element, the third chakra is the seat of ambition, drive, joy, and generosity. Just like the sun, it shines and brings warmth and happiness to the body and mind. When the solar plexus chakra is aligned and balanced, it leads to a feeling of stability, personal power, self-efficacy, and a connection to the authentic self. When this subtle energy is blocked, the opposite of bright and generous occurs, which may manifest as feelings of jealousy, greed, attempting to grip rather than give.[1] You may feel powerless and weak, doubting your abilities and feeling like an imposter.

How do you heal a blocked solar plexus chakra? There are various pranayama (breathing techniques) and yoga postures to assist with unblocking the chakras, but I'm going to focus on releasing blocks related to self-advocacy in the workplace. In Ayurveda, there is a basic principle around harmonizing and balancing imbalances in the mind and body: Like increases Like and Opposite decreases Same. If you are feeling constrained, feel tightness in areas of your body, or if you have a feeling of grasping with desperation, the perfect antidote to undo those unresourceful feelings would be doing the opposite. If you are feeling constrained, open up by taking up more space with your body. Breathe into any tight areas in the

---

[1]   Jade Doherty, The Art of Living (blog), "The Third Chakra: Your Personal Guide to Balance the Navel Chakra," June 18, 2021, https://www.artofliving.org/us-en/blog/the-third-chakra-your-personal-guide-to-balance-the-navel-chakra.

body and let go of the tight grasp. Letting go of a tight grasp can look like generosity or a sense of giving.

I worked with Nadia to use generosity as a portal to unblock her third chakra. Nadia, a Harvard graduate, works in one of the largest tech companies in the industry. She is a product manager for an initiative that could radically change the online educational space. She has been out of school for four years and is steadily climbing the corporate ladder. As she climbed, we worked through endless performance cycles and difficult team dynamics. I also coached her through her journey to advocate for other women of color on her team. Driven, ambitious, and motivated, her desire to succeed is unquestionable. She is so often focused on her personal success that she loses sight of the intensity that comes across to others. The bright light that illuminates so intently can also burn out and churn internally.

After a few consecutively canceled coaching sessions, I asked Nadia how she was feeling. She said she was experiencing extreme digestive issues and acid reflux. This was indication that we needed to nurse her solar plexus back to health. I suggested she increase her meditation practice and spend moments throughout the day focused on her mindfulness practice, using her breath as an anchor. I also suggested she do the following.

Deliberate Practice:
Balancing and Harmonizing the Solar Plexus Chakra

Step 1: Take a deep breath. As you inhale, lengthen the spine. As you exhale, bring your belly toward the spine as if you are giving yourself a hug with your abdomen. As you begin to deepen the breath, allow your mind to relax. Allow your thoughts to slow down.

Step 2: As you continue to breathe deeply through the abdomen, feel your feet grounded to the earth. If your legs are crossed, begin to uncross them. Ground your feet to the earth. Spread your toes out as wide as you can. Press into the balls and heels of the feet, and feel the support of the ground beneath you.

Step 3: In this balanced grounded state, think of someone on your team or in your organization that you know, someone who is junior to you and could use support. Ask yourself, "How can I advocate for them, mentor, or be of service to this person?"

Step 4: Schedule a meeting with this person, and ask how you can be of service. Support them generously.

When we partake in *seva* (selfless service), a principle rooted in the foundation of Sikhism, it takes the spotlight off of us and onto someone else with the intention to be of service. If you take a moment to consider how you can support someone and follow through with them, you can help others be bright, shining, radiant, lustrous gems. The solar plexus is the energy center of generosity. As you mentor or support someone on their career journey, help them speak up for themselves, or assist in helping them find their voice, it will allow the healing and unlocking of the unbalanced solar plexus. You will feel better about yourself, and you will help someone else in the process.

The fifth chakra is equally important to consider as it relates to self-advocacy. It explores all levels of communication with self and others and is associated with the Space element. *Vishuddha* translates to *especially pure*. The throat chakra governs communication with self, others, and our own higher power. When the throat chakra is balanced, we are able to tune in and listen to the guidance of our higher self. We can live our truth, pursue fulfilling work, and easily communicate with others with honesty and authenticity. When the throat chakra is imbalanced or blocked, communication breaks down with ourselves and others. We are unable to hear our own callings or desires and are dismissive of our higher self and intuition. Conversely, we are unable to truly hear and listen to others, which leads to a vicious cycle of inter- and intrapersonal conflict. This can manifest as an inability to clearly articulate emotions, lacking the vocabulary to describe feelings, and a consistent feeling of being misunderstood.

I have coached many women who struggle to speak their truth. Sandi, for example, was on an upward trajectory as a software engineer in a mid-sized tech company. She was really good at her job, yet she felt a big void in her life. Sandi loved teaching, so she found herself volunteering at a local prison to help inmates with math, a subject that came relatively easy to her. Unsure of her teaching skills, she experimented as a volunteer before leaving her job and pursing a new career as a teacher at a charter school. Leaving behind a comfortable salary, she felt more aligned to her purpose of helping and serving through education.

Sandi and I worked together for a few years as she experimented with different roles in the tech company. She constantly found herself in challenging interpersonal situations with her team. Feeling like an imposter, she struggled with speaking up when someone disagreed with her point of view. When we first met, I coached her on various NLP strategies to build rapport and communicate more effectively. The longer we worked together, the more obvious it became that the communication challenges were internal. She was not being honest with herself about her true desire to switch careers and focus on something that was more fulfilling for her.

How can you be an advocate or a cheerleader for yourself if you don't feel aligned and living a life that is true to your purpose?

I once experienced a similar dilemma when I graduated from college. I entered the world of consulting because I didn't know what else to do. I needed a paycheck, so I took the first job that came my way. After years of unfulfilling work, I noticed it was harder and harder to speak my truth because I wasn't even sure what was true for me. Returning to one of my true passions of psychology led me to pursue my master's degree in social and organizational psychology. This was my pure desire and the calling that opened the doors of adult learning, facilitation, and coaching. As I journey down the path that feels genuine and authentic for me, I find it easier to be my own cheerleader. I believe in myself and in the magnitude of my impact. When aligned, self-promotion doesn't feel like I am being salesy. I feel like I am speaking my truth and sharing my gifts in the world. It's much easier to grab the bullhorn for self-promotion when you speak your truth and are aligned with your purpose.

Deliberate Practice:
Living Your *Dharma*/Aligning the *Vishuddha* Chakra

Dharma is a Sanskrit word that translates to right direction or rightful duty. The concept refers to serving your true purpose or calling.

Step 1: Take a deep breath. As you inhale, lengthen the spine. As you exhale, bring your belly toward the spine as if you are giving yourself a hug with your abdomen. As you begin to deepen the breath, allow the mind to relax. Allow the thoughts to slow down.

Step 2: As you continue to breathe deeply through the abdomen, feel your feet grounded to the earth. If your legs are crossed, begin to uncross them. Ground your feet to the earth. Spread your toes out as wide as you can. Press into the balls and heels of the feet, and feel the support of the ground beneath you.

Step 3: In this balanced grounded state, ask yourself, "Am I doing what I am meant to be doing or on the path of fulfilling my true desire?"

If the answer is yes, consider what actions you want to take to expand and move further down the path. Do you need to continue your education, receive additional certifications, connect with specific people, or seek a mentor or coach?

If the answer is no, consider what other roles within your organization or externally that might be more aligned with your purpose. If you find yourself thinking of a different career, what might that path look like? With a curious mind and without judgment, allow yourself to travel internally and journal what arises. We are so quick to quiet our internal desires. There is no need to take action. Simply allow yourself to explore with genuine honesty and curiosity.

Step 4: To open the throat chakra, repeat affirmations that relate to authenticity and open communication. By repeating positive affirmations about authenticity, you create new thought patterns, behaviors, and actions that align with feelings of authenticity, self-expression, and living your *dharma*. Some examples include:

I communicate with ease.
I communicate my true desires with confidence.
I feel comfortable speaking my truth.
I am balanced in speaking and listening to myself.

CHAPTER 19

THE F WORD—THE ULTIMATE CLEANSING

"True forgiveness is when you say,
'Thank you for that experience.'"

—Oprah Winfrey

DURING EMOTIONAL TSUNAMIS (PROFESSIONAL OR personal), it's easy to lose sight of the fact that seeds of growth will emerge within the chaos. When you look back at these tumultuous times, such as being let go from a job, not getting the promotion you expected, or someone taking credit for your hard work, you may now realize that those experiences taught you the greatest lessons. How might you feel differently if you asked yourself, "What is my growing edge or the big lesson from this experience?" rather than "Why is this happening to me?" How might you have simultaneous awareness of the lesson(s) learned while also holding space for a better now and an even better future?

The answer is forgiveness. Without forgiveness, we cannot be relieved from the past. We are held captive by the person/people, the circumstance(s), or even our own behavior. In Buddhism, forgiveness is understood as a way to end suffering, to bring dignity and harmony into our life. Forgiveness is fundamentally for our own well-being and mental health. It is a way to let go of the pain we carry.

In social and organizational psychology, we take a systems approach when helping an individual navigate challenging terrain. If someone is disgruntled in their role at work, we look at the team and organizational dynamics to assess the situation. In Ayurveda, when someone complains of a finger ache, the entire arm or body is considered in the assessment. As such, I believe forgiveness can also be assessed from a systems approach.

Imagine the forgiveness system as an onion where the inner circle is Self. The outer layer represents Others (family group, friends, work colleagues, national group), and the outermost layer represents Global Group (everyone else).

Forgiveness System

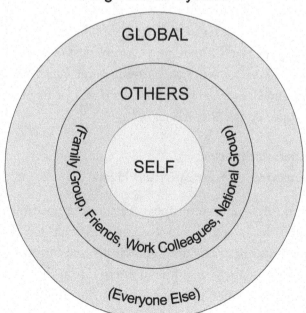

Research indicates that it's easier to forgive others than it is to forgive yourself. If someone has wronged you and they apologize, you can decide whether or not you want to forgive them. It's not such a clear path when you need to forgive yourself. Being able to forgive yourself requires empathy, compassion, kindness, and understanding. To forgive does not mean we condone the misdeeds of ourselves or others; it means we focus our energy to make sure the misdeeds never happen again. Without forgiveness, you will never release the sorrows of your past, and without collective-group forgiveness, we will not be released from the pain of past cultural wounds. The choice is absolutely yours: holding on to past pain or letting go with forgiveness.

When you reflect on your career thus far, there were likely many moments you didn't feel comfortable speaking up for yourself. Maybe you were silent when others took credit for your work, or perhaps you were overlooked for a well-deserved promotion. It's easy to beat yourself up and ruminate about the things you should have done or said, but it's in the past and grabbing the bullhorn for self-advocacy in the future requires forgiveness of yourself. Before we can forgive others, we must learn self-forgiveness. We can learn to forgive ourselves when we tap into the wellspring of love, resilience, and purity of our spiritual heart.

Deliberate Practice:
Connecting to Your Spiritual Heart

Step 1: Sit in a comfortable, cross-legged position on a cushion, or if you are in a chair, feel your feet firmly grounded to the floor. Feel your spine, tall but not rigid. Feel one straight strong line of energy from the crown of your head to your tailbone and from your tailbone to the crown of your head.

Step 2: When you feel ready, begin to gently close your eyes.

Step 3: You can relax the jaw and let the tongue rest in the pool of your lower mouth.

Step 4: Bring your attention and focus to the inhale. As you inhale, balloon the belly out. As you exhale, bring your belly toward the spine as if you are giving yourself a hug with the abdomen.

Step 5: Inhale, balloon the belly out. Exhale, belly in toward the spine.

Step 6: As you continue to breathe deeply and slowly, bring your attention and focus to your heart. Breathe into your physical heart.

Step 7: Now, bring your attention to the right side of your physical heart. On the right side of your physical heart is your spiritual heart. It's the size of a teardrop. Imagine a teardrop of divinity, universe, supreme consciousness, or God depending on whatever term resonates for you.

Step 8: As you breathe into this place of divinity within yourself, know that the impossible is possible. If it feels impossible to forgive yourself, notice what it feels like when you breathe into this teardrop of divinity. Imagine this teardrop expanding so much that you are able to travel inside, and in this place of purity and light, you can repeat these words, which are borrowed from Jack Kornfield[1]:

---

[1] Jack Kornfield, "Forgiveness Meditation," accessed October 2, 2021, https://jackkornfield.com/forgiveness-meditation/.

> I forgive myself for hurting and harming myself. I forgive myself for betraying or abandoning myself through thoughts, words, or deeds, knowingly or unknowingly. For the ways I have hurt myself through action or inaction, out of fear, pain, and confusion. I now extend a full and heartfelt forgiveness. I forgive myself. I forgive myself.

If you need to forgive yourself for harming others, you can repeat these words, which are also borrowed from Kornfield:

> I forgive myself for hurting and harming others. I forgive myself for betraying or abandoning others through thoughts, words, or deeds, knowingly or unknowingly. For the ways I have hurt others through action or inaction, out of fear, pain, and confusion. Picture each memory that still burdens your heart. And then to each person in your mind repeat: I ask for forgiveness; I ask for your forgiveness.

Forgiveness starts with the Self before we can move to the outer layers of the onion. If the outer layer of Others (family, friends, work colleagues) has hurt or harmed us in anyway, we must move through the same process.

Deliberate Practice:
Connecting to Your Spiritual Heart to Forgive Others for Hurting or Harming You

Step 1: Sit in a comfortable, cross-legged position on a cushion, or if you are in a chair, feel your feet firmly grounded to the floor. Feel your spine, tall but not rigid.

Feel one straight strong line of energy from the crown of your head to your tailbone and from your tailbone to the crown of your head.

Step 2: When you feel ready, begin to gently close your eyes.

Step 3: You can relax your jaw and let the tongue rest in the pool of your lower mouth.

Step 4: Bring your attention and focus to the inhale. As you inhale, balloon the belly out. As you exhale, bring your belly toward the spine as if you are giving yourself a hug with the abdomen.

Step 5: Inhale, balloon the belly out. Exhale, belly in toward the spine.

Step 6: As you continue to breathe deeply and slowly, bring your attention and focus to your heart. Breathe into your physical heart.

Step 7: Now, bring your attention to the right side of your physical heart. On the right side of your physical heart is your spiritual heart. It's the size of a teardrop. Imagine it's a teardrop of divinity, universe, supreme consciousness, or God depending on whatever term resonates for you.

Step 8: As you breathe into this place of divinity within yourself, know that the impossible is possible. Notice what it feels like as you breathe into this teardrop of divinity. Imagine this teardrop expanding so much that you are able to travel inside, and in this place of purity and light, you can repeat these words, which are borrowed from Jack Kornfield:

There are many ways that I have been harmed by others, abused, or abandoned, knowingly or unknowingly, in thought, word, or deeds. I now remember the many ways others have hurt or harmed me, wounded me, out of fear, pain, confusion, and anger. I have carried this pain in my heart too long. I offer forgiveness. To the groups who have caused me and my ancestor's harm, I offer my forgiveness. I forgive you.

Given the current climate of national and global affairs amidst the COVID-19 pandemic, it's easy to hold anger, aggression, and resentment toward national and global leadership. If ever there is a time to practice forgiveness to the powers that be, it would be now. In my mind, I believe ancestral trauma or wrongdoings fall in the global group, the outermost layer. To move on from individual and ancestral trauma, we must forgive.

Whether you are Asian or South Asian, you are well aware of the personal and family perfectionism that is embedded within our cultures. We may have had to behave a certain way or refrain from saying how we felt for fear of what others would think about our families. Maybe we began a career that wasn't what our heart desired because it's what was expected. Perhaps we didn't see the women in our lives advocating for themselves. Whatever the case may be for you, there is forgiveness required from all of us of the perfectionist tendencies embedded within our cultural roots.

Deliberate Practice:
Connecting to Your Spiritual Heart to
Forgive Others (National and Global
Groups) for Hurting or Harming You

Step 1: Sit in a comfortable, cross-legged position on a cushion, or if you are in a chair, feel your feet firmly grounded to the floor. Feel your spine, tall but not rigid. Feel one straight strong line of energy from the crown of your head to your tailbone and from your tailbone to the crown of your head.

Step 2: When you feel ready, begin to gently close your eyes.

Step 3: You can relax your jaw and let the tongue rest in the pool of your lower mouth.

Step 4: Bring your attention and focus to the inhale. As you inhale, balloon the belly out. As you exhale, bring your belly toward the spine as if you are giving yourself a hug with the abdomen.

Step 5: Inhale, balloon the belly out. Exhale, belly in toward the spine.

Step 6: As you continue to breathe deeply and slowly, bring your attention and focus to your heart. Breathe into your physical heart.

Step 7: Now, bring your attention to the right side of your physical heart. On the right side of your physical heart is your spiritual heart. It's the size of a teardrop. Imagine it's a teardrop of divinity, universe, supreme consciousness, or God depending on whatever term resonates for you. In the spiritual heart, we are all connected. There is no other.

Step 8: As you breathe into this place of divinity within yourself, know that the impossible is possible. Notice what it feels like as you breathe into this teardrop of divinity. Imagine this teardrop expanding so much that you are able to travel inside, and in this place of purity and light, you can repeat these words, which are borrowed from Jack Kornfield:

> There are many ways that I have been harmed by others, abused, or abandoned, knowingly or unknowingly, in thought, word, or deeds. I now remember the many ways others have hurt or harmed me, wounded me, out of fear, pain, confusion, and anger. I have carried this pain in my heart too long. I offer forgiveness. To those who have caused me harm, I offer my forgiveness. I forgive you.

CLOSING

AS I CONCLUDE, I'D LIKE to thank you for taking a journey of self-promotion and self-advocacy with me. These practices are always available to you, whether you are starting your career, in the middle, or close to retirement. Whether you read this book because you were searching for tools to be your own cheerleader or because you coach and mentor younger Asian and South Asian women, I'm grateful that you chose to spend your time and energy exploring my thoughts and learning from my experiences.

As you continue this journey of grabbing the bullhorn for yourself or modeling this behavior for other women, I will leave you with a final thought regarding self-compassion. Without self-compassion, we will not be able to move through difficult conversations, ask for the promotions we deserve, or speak up when there is a wrongdoing. Dr. Kristin Neff states, "Compassion can be ferocious as well as tender." Tender compassion is loving, kind, and gentle, whereas ferocious self-compassion is when you speak up with confidence because an injustice has occurred. The ferocity comes in letting go of the familiar pattern of staying silent and speaking your truth. Like the mama bear who protects her cub, you are the mama bear of yourself. You are the protector and communicator of your truth.

According to Dr. Neff, there are three components of self-compassion: mindfulness, common humanity, and kindness. I close with a final practice of fierce self-compassion that will be required as you grab the bullhorn to be your own cheerleader.

Deliberate Practice:
Practicing Fierce Self-Compassion (Borrowed from
Dr. Kristin Neff's Fierce Self-Compassion Break)[1]

Step 1: Think of a situation where you need to protect yourself, draw boundaries, or stand up for yourself. Maybe you are in a situation at work where you are feeling taken advantage of, or you are being treated unfairly. Maybe there is something happening that is unjust, and you want to stop it.

Step 2: Recollect the situation in your mind's eye. See what you see, hear what you hear, and feel what you feel as you remember the situation. What are you experiencing? Fear, anger, or frustration? What sensations are you experiencing in your body?

Step 3: Make contact with the discomfort as a physical sensation in the body. Where is it located? What is the texture, temperature, or rhythm? Notice what you notice.

Step 4: Bring in the three components of self-compassion so you can protect yourself.

> » Mindfulness:
>
>> o Say out loud, "I clearly see the truth of what's happening." Other options may be: "This is not okay," "I'm not safe," or "This is unfair." Use the language that best works for you.

---

1   "Fierce Self-Compassion Resources," accessed September 29, 2021, https://greatergood.berkeley.edu/images/uploads/Neff_Fierce_Self-Compassion_Resources.pdf.

» Common Humanity:

○ Say out loud, "I am not alone. I am among many other Asian and South Asian women." Another option might be, "I am not a victim; I am empowered."

» Self-Kindness

○ Bringing your fist over your heart as a gesture of strength and power, say out loud, "I will protect myself." Another option is, "I will take whatever action is necessary to prevent this!"

Step 5: If you are having difficulty finding the right words, imagine that someone you really care about is being mistreated or taken advantage of the exact same way you are. What would you say to this person to help them be strong, stand up for themselves, and speak their truth? Now you can offer the same message to yourself.

Step 6: Put your other hand over your fist and hold it tenderly. This tenderness merges with the ferocity of the fist. Give yourself permission to feel the force of the ferocity of the anger or resolve and simultaneously feel the loving embrace the other hand provides over the fist. Aim your fierce compassion at the harm or injustice, not at the person causing the harm. They are human, and you are human. Call on the ferocity to take action, while keeping the thread of tender self-love alive.

LETTER TO THE READER

Dear Reader,

From very early on in my life, I remember feeling anxious. I didn't have a label for it, but I remember feeling as if I was trying to get out of quicksand and couldn't breathe. I only realized in adulthood that I suffered from panic attacks. I endured years of performance anxiety from test taking in school coupled with being bullied and beaten up regularly for being different. My breaking point came in 2004.

After an abrupt ending to an unhealthy marriage in which I succumbed to cultural pressures, I knew I needed to find help. By abrupt, I mean I walked out after a couple of short months. I had nowhere to go and no idea how to find support. I didn't feel safe going to the Gurdwara (Sikh temple) because I felt so much shame. It was the first time in my life that I didn't feel like I was part of a community. I was truly an *I*, and no longer part of any *We*.

In hindsight, becoming an *I* was exactly what I needed to set me on the path to fulfill my dharma (life purpose). It was in those dark times that I found therapy and delved deep into different modes of holistic health and wellness.

I needed a shoulder to cry on, and I found it at the Art of Living Retreat Center.[1] I began going to *satsangs* (spiritual discourse and sacred gatherings) where I learned the *Sudarshan Kriya*, a unique breathing practice that involves cyclical breathing patterns that range from slow and calming to rapid and stimulating. I listened intently to the teachings of Sri Ravi Shankar, founder of the Art of Living, and felt a warm hug from the community. No one asked me what I was going through. They would only ask me if I was okay when they saw me getting emotional after the *kriyas*. This community helped me get back on my feet. I even had the opportunity to attend a couple of *satsangs* with Sri Ravi Shankar. He walked by me, saw me tear up, and put his hand on my head and said, "God bless you, my child." This was the moment of my spiritual awakening—a moment that is etched in my memory and will remain with me until I leave this body.

Some cosmic conscious energy awakened, and it led me to explore meditation, pranayama (breathing exercises), yoga, and Ayurveda. I was rapidly consuming spiritual books by Esther and Jerry Hicks, Dr. Wayne Dyer, Dr. Michael Beckwith, Deepak Chopra, Dr. Vasant Lad, Eckhart Tolle, Neale Donald Walsch, and Marianne Williamson, to name a few. I couldn't get enough. I needed answers to questions that I'd had as a small child when I'd ask my mom what my life purpose was.

---

1   https://artoflivingretreatcenter.org/

Around the same time, I started seeing a therapist and have continued to seek support as needed for over sixteen years.

My desire for continuous learning and personal development led me to complete my master's degree in social and organizational psychology. I became a yoga teacher with numerous certifications, an Ayurveda specialist, and an NLP Coach & Master Practitioner. I am always open to learning different modes of healing that will help me and all of the clients I serve. There is no magic pill to feel happy or experience joy. It takes a cocktail of modalities working congruently to achieve mental health and well-being. I draw from practices from many religions, spiritual traditions, and neuroscience practices to keep me grounded and rooted to my center. Thanks to these practices and healing work over the years, my panic attacks have subsided, and if I do feel emotionally overwhelmed, I have many tools in my toolkit to get through the challenging moment(s).

As I reflect, when I left my marriage, it was the first time in my life that I stood up for myself. It was the first time that I didn't think of the repercussions—I knew my truth in that moment. It is my first memory of being my own cheerleader. It took being my own cheerleader personally to open the door to be my own cheerleader professionally. I didn't know how to flex the self-advocacy muscle as a child, teenager, or young adult, and there are times when I still struggle with it. It is a life-long journey.

Be Your Own Cheerleader is rooted and inspired by my own personal experimentation and exploration with NLP, yoga, Ayurveda, mindfulness, and meditation. I was my own first client, and now, fifteen years later, I have helped thousands of people, including hundreds of Asian and South Asian women, be their own cheerleaders personally and professionally.

My hope is that this book inspires you to be your own cheerleader in all aspects of your life. I focus specifically on work, but self-advocacy and self-promotion is a muscle that can only be developed if we practice daily with friends, family, and partners in addition to colleagues and bosses.

Warmly,

Neelu Kaur

ACKNOWLEDGMENTS

I'D LIKE TO THANK MY folks, (Manjit Singh and Narinder Kaur). I wouldn't have been able to write this book without all of the experiences that were afforded to me because of their sacrifices.

Thank you to my earliest memories of cheerleaders—Ashish Tagra and Trudi Fiscarelli.

Thank you to all of my many teachers, friends, and cheerleaders along the way. A special thank you to Charlotte Taft, who has been one of my biggest supporters for the past fifteen years. Kaity Leisure, Xai Moua, and Dr. Linda Pittenger for your endless faith in my ability to write this book.

Dr. Lee Knefelkamp was one of my dear professors in graduate school at Columbia University. She created a safe space for me to be vulnerable and radically accept my true, authentic self.

Thank you to Rachel Hott and Steven Leeds from the NLP Center of New York for all of your NLP teachings and wisdom.

I took nuggets of wisdom and insights from the ancient wisdom and teachings from Ayurveda, yoga, Sikhism, Buddhism, and Hinduism. The teachings and literature from social and organizational psychology and NLP laid the foundation for *Be Your Own Cheerleader*.

I am so grateful and honored to the organizations and individuals who hired me to teach, facilitate, and coach over the years, which provided me with experiences to share with you in this book.

The Highlights Foundation provided the writer's retreat where I began the journey of writing *Be Your Own Cheerleader*.

Thank you for your guidance throughout the writing and publishing process: Colleen Darby, Katie Mathur, Howard Cohen, and Philip Laughlin.

Thank you to Kat Pedersen (Book Coach & Editor), Harvey Klinger (Literary Agent), Debra Englander (Editor), Heather King (Managing Editor), and everyone else at Post Hill Press (Publisher) who supported me through the publishing process. Without all of you, this book would not have made it onto the shelves and into the hands of readers.

This book was the interweaving and stitching of so many pieces of brilliant research from the following:

Geert Hofstede
Shelle Rose Charvet
Dr. Dan Siegel
Dr. Lisa Feldman Barrett
Dr. Amy Cuddy
Wendy Palmer
Dr. Marilee Adams
Byron Katie
Pia Mellody
Rev. Michael Beckwith
Pema Chödrön
Noah St. John
Dr. Vasant Lad
Dr. Marc Halpern
Jack Kornfield
Dr. Kristin Neff

Lastly, to all the naysayers, I learned so much from you.

Appendix

I

MANAGING BIAS AND EIGHT STRATEGIES TO SPEAK UP

ADAPTED FROM *PROMOTING DIVERSITY AND Social Justice (2nd edition)* by Diane J. Goodman. 2011.

1. "The Echo": Paraphrase or repeat back what they said. By rephrasing what the other person said, you make sure you understand what they said, and it gives the other person the opportunity to reflect on what they said. The tone of voice is important. You're not trying to ridicule, just trying to understand and clarify.

2. "The Questionator": Ask for more information. This strategy is a great way to help you understand why they said what they said, and again, it gives the person another chance to reflect on what they said. After saying it again, they might realize their statement doesn't make sense or is unfounded. Being genuine is important. Shaming or using sarcasm can backfire.

3. "The Huh?": Play dumb. Another way to get them to reflect on what they said—especially good for responding to jokes. You can ask them why race, gender, sexual orientation, religion, nationality, disability, etc. is rele-

vant to the story or ask them to explain the meaning of a specific slur or derogatory term.

4.   "The Debunker": Challenge the stereotype. Offer another side of the story by challenging the assumption or stereotype. Use your personal experiences and knowledge to show how the stereotype presented isn't valid.

5.   "The Connector": Highlight commonalities. Comments based on bias and prejudice create an us-versus-them situation. Highlighting the ways in which the person making the comments is the same as the subject of the comment can help dial down the otherness.

6.   "The Emoter": Express your feelings. Tell the person how you feel and why. Then offer a more appropriate alternative.

7.   "The I've Been There": Share your own process. Without sounding self-righteous, talk about how you used to think the same, but you've changed. Explain what made you change your views.

8.   "The One-Worder": Say "Ouch." Sometimes when the comment is directed at you personally, you want to respond immediately but can't think of a good response. Saying "ouch" can stop the person making the comment and lets them know that what they said was hurtful. It's a safe, simple strategy that can work well in casual, peer-to-peer situations.

GLOBAL CROSS-COUNTRY POWER DISTANCE INDEX (PDI) SCORES

Source: https://www.hofstede-insights.com/country-comparison/
THIS IS A SAMPLE OF Asian and South Asian countries compared with the United States on their PDI scores.

1. Comparing China, India, Thailand, and the United States, the Asian and South Asian countries' PDI scores are substantially higher than those of the United States.

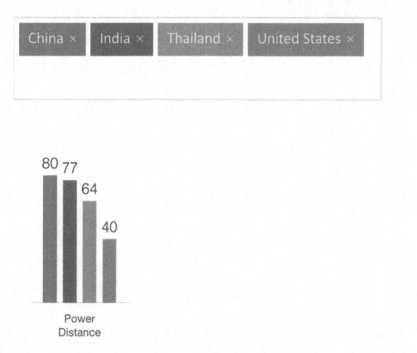

China ×   India ×   Thailand ×   United States ×

80 77
64
40

Power
Distance

2. Comparing Bangladesh, the Philippines, Vietnam, and the United States, the Asian and South Asian PDI scores are substantially higher than those of the United States.

Bangladesh ×   Philippines ×   United States ×

Vietnam ×

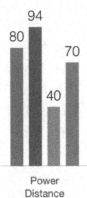

Power
Distance

3. Comparing Indonesia, Japan, Pakistan, and the United States, the Asian and South Asian PDI Scores are substantially higher than those of the United States.

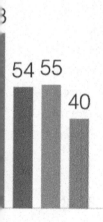

54 55

40

Power
Distance

III

AYURVEDA

AYURVEDA IS ONE OF THE holistic systems of healing that allows me to take care of myself so I can grab the bullhorn when I need it. This Indian-based healing system dates back 5,000 years and offers ancient wisdom that applies in the modern day.

I've taken this Eastern approach and coupled it with Western research in the fields of neuroscience and sleep hygiene to create daily and evening routines that bring radical change to the body, mind, and consciousness. Routines can help you find balance, harmony, discipline, peace, happiness, and longevity, leading to an increased self-esteem which is necessary when it comes to self-advocacy, speaking up, and grabbing the bullhorn every day at work.

There are many habits or routines covered below. The intention of this list is not to overwhelm you but to provide many options you can experiment with to tap into your well-being, so you can bring your full powerful self to work every day.

MORNING ROUTINES THAT HELP JUMPSTART THE BRAIN:

1. Wake Up with the Sun: Sunlight helps regulate melatonin production in the body, which is necessary to maintain circadian rhythms. Melatonin is an essential hormone released by the pineal gland in the brain. This hormone regulates the sleep-wake cycle. Getting at least fifteen minutes of sunlight exposure helps regulate mel-

atonin, provides calcium absorption, and helps promote the synthesis of vitamin D3.

2.	Hydrate: Drink two cups of room temperature water to cleanse the system. Our brain is comprised of approximately 80 percent water. In other words, three quarters of our brain is water. Even slight dehydration can cause fatigue, headaches, lack of mental clarity, stress, and sleep issues. We lose a lot of water while we sleep, so hydrate first thing in the morning.

3.	Brush Teeth with the Non-Dominant Hand: Using your non-dominant hand will strengthen neural connections in the brain and even create new ones. Research indicates that when we use our non-dominant hand for tasks, it can result in thinking differently and becoming more creative problem-solvers.

4.	Go Device-Free for the First Hour of Your Day: Research indicates that the first hour of the day sets the tone for the entire day. If you reach for your phone first thing in the morning, you are training your brain to be reactive and distracted all day. You might be tempted to respond to emails, get lost in doom-scrolling, or binge on social media, which can affect your mood for the entire day. If an hour seems too difficult, try thirty minutes and eventually work your way up to an hour.

5.	Brainpower Smoothie: There are certain foods that are excellent for brain health. You can make a smoothie with leafy greens, blueberries, turmeric, ginger, and avocados. If your diet permits, wild salmon and dark chocolate are also considered brain foods.

6.   Movement: Anything that is good for the heart is good for the brain. This doesn't mean you need to do a full workout in the morning. You can do a few rounds of *Surya Namaskar* (sun salutations) or take a leisurely stroll.[1]

AYURVEDIC MORNING ROUTINES:

1.   Gratitude or Prayer: Start your day with a prayer or gratitude, appreciating that you are on this earth. Try a simple mantra, such as "May love, peace, joy, and abundance be a part of my life and all those around me on this day." It can be something simple that resonates with you. Starting your day on a positive note sets the tone for the entire day.

2.   Evacuation: After drinking two glasses of room temperature water, a regular bowel movement is an indicator of overall health because healthy elimination points to a strong *agni* (digestive fire), which is one of the cornerstones of well-being and longevity.

3.   Scrape Your Tongue: Gently scape the tongue from the back forward for at least 7–14 strokes. This stimulates the internal organs, helps digestion, and removes toxins in the body. (For information on the best types of tongue scrapers, visit the Ayurvedic Institute https://www.ayurveda.com/.)

4.   Nasal Drops (*Nasya*): Put 3–5 drops of warm oil or ghee (clarified butter from the milk of a cow) into each nostril in the morning. This helps lubricate the nose, clean the sinuses, and improve voice, vision, and mental clarity. The nose is the doorway to the brain, so nose drops

---

1   https://en.wikipedia.org/wiki/Sun_Salutation

are said to bring intelligence and nourish the mind. (For information on the types of oils to use, visit the Ayurvedic Institute https://www.ayurveda.com/.)

5. Oil Drops in the Ears (*Karana Purana*): Putting 3–5 drops of warm sesame oil in each ear helps with conditions such as ringing ears, excess, ear wax, poor healing, and Temporomandibular Joint (TMJ) disorders.

6. Apply Oil to the Head and Body (*Abhyanga*): Rubbing warm oil to the scalp and body is an act of self-love. Starting your day with warm oil is nourishing for the body and soul. It helps with stress management and brings about a sense of balance and harmony.

7. Yoga: Yoga helps improve circulation, strength, flexibility, and endurance. Yoga helps improve digestion and elimination. In the morning, you can start with a few rounds of *Surya Namaskar* (Sun Salutations) and build up to 10–12 rounds. (For specifics on pace and rhythm, visit the Ayurvedic Institute at https://www.ayurveda.com/.)

8. Pranayama/Breathing Exercises: Prana represents the physical forces of light, heat, and energy. Breathing exercises help to improve mental well-being. A strong practice is believed to help detoxify the body while strengthening the respiratory system. After your movement practice, sit quietly and practice pranayama. (For specifics on the types of breathing exercises, visit the Ayurvedic Institute at https://www.ayurveda.com/.)

9. Meditation: Meditating for 15–20 minutes every day has been scientifically proven to lower blood pressure and relieve depression and anxiety. Meditation brings your focus to the here and now, and whether you use a guided

meditation, a meditation app, or your breath, you are training your brain to return to the present moment.

AYURVEDIC EVENING ROUTINES:

1. Dinner: Prepare and eat a light, easy-to-digest meal at least three hours before bedtime. The *agni* (digestive fire) is said to be at its peak at noon, so it's best to eat your largest meal during lunch and your lightest meal at dinner. It's harder to fall and stay asleep if you eat too close to bedtime. Sleep will be disturbed and not as restful if you go to bed with a full stomach.

2. Pamper Hour: The hour before bedtime is ideally a time of leisurely activities. This is an hour to unwind from the day. Reading with lights coming from over the shoulders and not directly in the eyes helps the melatonin production in the body. The hour before bed should not be a time to pay bills or deal with serious matters. It is a conflict-free hour with no news and ideally no devices.

3. Massage Head, Scalp, and Feet: Rubbing sesame or coconut oil on your head, scalp, and feet can help to relax the body. It has a calming effect of bringing the energy levels down for improved sleep.

4. Aromatherapy: You can diffuse calming essential oils like lavender, chamomile, sandalwood, or jasmine, to name a few, or add them to your massage oil. These calming scents can help relax the body and mind and prepare for restful sleep.

5. Prayers, Meditation, or Gratitude: Settling the mind down before bed can help with restful sleep. Whether it's mantra, a few minutes of silence, or gratitude for all

of your blessings, these practices will help you transition from your day into a restorative night's sleep.

SLEEP HYGIENE:

1. Melatonin and Lighting: Darkness prompts the pineal gland to start producing melatonin while light causes that production to stop. Melatonin helps regulate circadian rhythm and synchronize the sleep-wake cycle with night and day. Because lighting affects the production of melatonin, it's best to have a night light in the bathroom. I even use the nightlight instead of the big lights when washing my face and brushing my teeth. If you get up once or often to use the bathroom, it's best to keep the night light on and use that instead of the big overhead light.

2. Keep It Cool: Your body temperature needs to drop its core temperature by about 2–3 degrees Fahrenheit to fall and stay asleep. Research indicates that the best temperature to fall asleep is 60–67 degrees Fahrenheit (15.6 to 19.4 degrees Celsius).

3. Regularity with Sleep: Fall asleep and wake up at one set time every day. Your body's internal clock follows a specific sleep-wake cycle. Going to bed late one night and early the next throws your circadian rhythm off balance. According to Dr. Matthew Walker, attempting to catch up on missed sleep over the weekend may not always be effective and can result in physical and mental fatigue. Adhering to a daily sleep schedule can be beneficial for your overall health and well-being.

4. Twenty-Minute Rule + Creative Imagery: According to the Manhattan Sleep Clinic, lying in bed for prolonged

periods of time isn't an effective sleep strategy. Your brain will associate anxiety and being awake with your bed. If you cannot fall asleep for twenty minutes, get out of bed and do a relaxing activity until you start feeling sleepy. A calming activity that helps during periods of troubled sleep is called creative imagery. You may picture a relaxing vacation or a peaceful place you like to visit. Imagine each and every detail with a prolonged breath. In this creative imagery, you are alone with no distractions. You allow your mind to focus on each and every detail. For example, if you are at a beach, you imagine the sand between your toes, the warmth of the sun on your skin and the wind breeze through your hair. While you focus on each calming detail, you take deep, long abdominal breaths.

5. Optimize the Book Ends / Sleep Divorce: Because sleep is so important, Dr. Matthew Walker suggests a sleep divorce to avoid a real divorce. If you cannot sleep soundly with your partner by your side, optimize the book ends. Connect before bedtime and in the morning, but separate to sleep.

In summary, here's a quick, easy list to remember the "Rule of Five" that blends Eastern and Western recommendations for sleep best practices:

1. Wake up and Sleep at 1 Set Time
2. No Caffeine after 2pm
3. No Food 3 hours before Bedtime
4. No Exercise 4 hours before Bedtime
5. High 5 the Sun—Wake up with the Sun

To learn more about Ayurveda, below are resources that provide additional details about daily, evening, and seasonal self-care routines:

1. The Ayurvedic Institute: https://www.ayurveda.com/

2. MAPI: https://mapi.com/pages/about-ayurveda

3. Banyan Botanicals: https://www.banyan-botanicals.com/info/ayurvedic-living/learning-ayurveda/intro-to-ayurveda/

4. The Chopra Center: https://chopra.com/articles/ayurveda

ABOUT THE AUTHOR

Author photo: Irina Peschan, IrinaPeschan.com

NEELU KAUR IS A FACILITATOR, Neuro-linguistic Programming (NLP) Executive Coach and Burnout Management Specialist. She holds a bachelor's degree from New York University Stern School of Business and a master's degree in social and organizational psychology from Columbia University and is a certified NLP Coach and Master Practitioner from the NLP Center of New York. Neelu has fifteen years of experience specializing in adult learning and leadership development in large organizations ranging from financial services and consulting to the tech industry. She is a certified yoga instructor, Ayurveda specialist, and an Ericksonian-trained hypnotherapist focused on bringing mindfulness and stress management practices to individuals, teams, and organizations. Neelu and her extensive book collection reside in Forest Hills, Queens, New York.